The Insider's Guide to

# Writing for Television

## Julian Friedmann
### and
## Christopher Walker

I0414085

trotman t

**Also in this series**

*The Insider's Guide to Getting Your Book Published*

*The Insider's Guide to Writing for Television*

This first edition published in 2012 by Trotman Publishing, an imprint of Crimson Publishing Ltd, Westminster House, Kew Road, Richmond, Surrey, TW9 2ND

British Library Cataloguing in Publication Data
A catalogue record for this book is available from the British Library

ISBN 978 1 84455 376 1

Typeset by IDSUK (DataConnection) Ltd
Printed and bound in the UK by Ashford Colour Press, Gosport, Hants

# Contents

Contents

# The art and craft of writing for television audiences 119

# Foreword

Perhaps you bought this book because you have been thinking about becoming a screenwriter for some time. Maybe you haven't had a chance to get anything down on paper or computer screen. You're undecided about what sort of story to tell. Are you a romantic or a horror-meister? Are you Julian Fellowes or Steven Moffat? Perhaps you feel you need to conduct more research, to find out what the television industry is looking for – what genres are trending?

Well I'm sorry but already I'm suspicious.

Writers may often research their work but they rarely research their desire to work. Writing should be more than an itch one needs to scratch; it should be a way of relating to the world that one simply cannot ignore or avoid. Putting it simply, you should be writing already. That's where to begin. At the desk. In front of the Mac. Crazy ideas spilling out of your head. Sploshing across the screen like wet paint. Laying it down like Jackson Pollock with nary a care in the world. Being a writer isn't what you do, it's who you are.

It's frightening, sending your work into an uncaring world. There is no reason for people to like or connect with your script. There are so many scripts out there – how the hell is yours going to stand out? No answer to that, apart from the obvious – with talent and a smidgen of amazing luck. But you cannot let that put you off. It all must start with You. What You want to write about. What story matters to You. Some will call that confidence and others will label it hubris. And then if it reaches development or even production you will be bombarded by notes from all sides – actors, editors, producers, directors, TV execs – all challenging your work, pulling it in different directions. Who do you listen to? When do you concede and when do you stand your ground? Again, there is no easy straight answer. And finally when your baby steps out onto the screen you will hear a cold hard voice bellow 'release the creatures!' And out of the fetid bowels of Hades will crawl The Critics. And God only knows what garlands or thunderbolts they will hurl at your head.

This book is not a panacea for the trials, tribulations and joys of screenwriting. It is a road-map through the terrain. It cannot cross the misty mountains for you but it can tell you where they are to be found and which walking boots to wear for them. It combines advice on how to corral that unruly imagination of yours with a practical guide to finding those precious champions within the business who can help move you forward. What it cannot do – what no book can do – is turn a non-writer into a writer. I've sometimes heard people musing, 'I might get into the writing game. I hear there's money in it'. Those people do not succeed. But you sploshers of wet undisciplined paint – and you know who you are – *you* are who this book is written for.

Enjoy it. Learn from it. Be inspired by it. And keep on sploshing.

Matthew Graham
January 2012

# Introduction

If you are reading this, you are presumably serious about writing for television. Perhaps you already write for television and want to improve your career or perhaps you write in other media and want to see if television is where you should be focusing your efforts. Or perhaps you're a complete beginner who loves watching television and has a fantastic idea for a new show (or for developing an existing one). If you fall into any of these three categories, this book is for you.

*The Insider's Guide to Writing for Television* is unlike other writing guides in two important respects. Firstly, it concentrates solely on television scriptwriting, which is quite different from writing for the theatre or the cinema, both in terms of craft and career development. Secondly, it offers expert advice in both those distinct areas: craft *and* career development. Being a talented writer is not enough. If you want to make a living writing for television you need to be a successful businessperson too and this book will help you master both sets of skills.

The first section of the book, written by Julian Friedmann, is concerned with the business of writing for television, and offers strategies for breaking into the industry and subsequently making a living. It covers everything from research and training to putting together a submission package to negotiating contracts.

The second section, written by Christopher Walker, discusses the art and craft of writing for television audiences, and provides creative advice on producing scripts that will sell in today's crowded, fast-moving marketplace. It covers format and genre as well as how to produce the industry's selling documents, the synopsis, treatment and scene-by-scene breakdown.

No prior knowledge is assumed, but we hope the experienced writer will also find much of value in this book. It is intended to remain a trusted companion throughout your writing life, taken down from the shelf and consulted again each time your career takes another exciting step forward.

# The business of writing for television

# Part One
## Breaking in

# 1 Why write for television?

How writing for TV compares with writing for other media, and why you need to be a businessperson as well as a writer

## The business of writing for television

Writers are usually freelancers, with all the connotations of irregular income and eking out a livelihood. Many writers are driven by a desire to tell stories. They do not see writing primarily in terms of bringing in money but rather as something they have to do. For some, storytelling in whatever format is almost a compulsion.

Most writers, whether experienced, compulsive or beginners, do not see themselves as running a 'business' and, as a result, do not behave in a businesslike way. They allow themselves to be disadvantaged, with the result that they earn below the minimum wage. They put themselves into that position and cannot blame producers – some of whom are equally impoverished – for exploiting them.

Committed writers tend to keep going whether they earn from their writing or not and one must have some admiration for them, especially if they also have talent. Yet some with talent do not always carve out for themselves the career that they want, though there are always others – with less talent – who do manage to achieve a career. Which are you likely to be?

Many experienced scriptwriters will admit that they spend more time rewriting than writing. As you will see, scriptwriters (more than novelists) get feedback, notes and criticism from many people. Often the feedback is contradictory: not everyone will respond to the treatment or script in the same way (the treatment is a relatively short prose document outlining what the script will be about, possibly including the structure of the story).

Dealing with good notes, bad notes, and even silly notes is all part of the job of being a professional writer. This too common experience of the difficult process of developing the story from idea into treatment and then into script is sometimes called 'development hell'. It is common for a produced script to have been rewritten a dozen or more times (not necessarily every page is rewritten every time). There are ways of limiting or lessening the need for unnecessary rewrites, which will be explained in Chapters 3 and 4.

Nevertheless, there is a marketplace for television writers and this section of the book explains what it is and how best to get into it and build a better career. It shows you that there are certain things that writers can do to be more businesslike about their careers, and there are many things – including not giving up the day job too early or finding a part-time job – that can ease the financial situation. Equally important are the choices that writers make, choices about everything from genre and format to training, and when to give up that day job. Such decisions can be the basis for building a career and a small business and are as relevant as understanding the specific income tax allowances for writers.

It is worth noting that many of the scripts that agents and producers have sent to them appear to have been written with little thought about what is likely to sell. On the other hand, some of the greatest scripts written were not written with the market in mind. So it is not obvious how to build a career as a professional writer and arguably today it is tougher than ever to do so.

The days when beginner-writers could easily target the relatively easy-access television soaps and series as the way to gain credits and some income have more or less gone mainly because there are fewer such series being made.

An additional route we would encourage is that of short films (usually between 5–10 minutes but they can be as long as 30 minutes) which enable the writer's voice to be heard (this cannot be said of the soaps, where your ability to 'get' the voice of well-known and much-loved characters is one of the important attributes that leads to a career).

As this is a book about writing for television, there will not be much on writing for the big screen, for radio or theatre and it is important to understand the basic differences between these formats. It is also important to understand that it can be easier to get writing credits in radio or in the theatre than in film or television.

## Writing for radio

Radio is often thought of as a good place for beginners to start and for experienced writers to go to as well. Risks will often be taken with newer writers. However, never send a failed television script with a note saying that you think it will work well on radio. You have to write it as if it were a radio script. Check Google or the archives of www.twelvepoint.com for articles about writing for radio.

## Writing for film

It is important to understand the differences between writing a single drama for television and a feature film. In the past, one looked at the following criteria to determine whether a script would be best suited for a feature film.

- **Does it need 'the big screen'?**

  Is it a story that needs the big screen to show it to the best effect (are there epic scenes, great vistas, fast-paced action, big emotions)? Is it a genre that will attract large enough audiences to induce investors to back the usually higher-budget feature film? There are a number of articles on this subject in the archive of www.twelvepoint.com or elsewhere on the web.

- **How much will it cost to create?**

  Because of the new generations of very small and light high-definition cameras, it is possible to shoot a feature film with a tiny crew and edit it on a home computer with brilliant software. Ten years ago a high-value television drama for primetime would probably have cost between £600,000 and £900,000 (some would be more). In the last five years there have been some exceptional, full-length feature films made for less than £100,000.

Writers need to know in broad terms what the costs of a script are likely to be: how to keep the below-the-line costs down and why the above-the-line costs can be variable. Above-the-line covers cast, writer and director and the main producer's fees; below-the-line is everything else.

- **Are the lead roles good enough?**

  A key element missing in the majority of scripts that agents see arriving on their desks is that the leading roles are not roles that actors and their agents will fight to have. The actors in *Four Weddings and a Funeral* readily played their roles because the script – for a television movie (which is what it was) – was excellent. Few of them realised how the film would change their careers.

If a script intended for a small film, perhaps a television movie, is so good that it attracts expensive stars, the budget will obviously go up; the movie industry is star-led and it is stars who attract finance. So if a below £1m budget was intended but a couple of A-list stars fall in love with the script and each of them will cost £1m, the film may be easier to finance at £3m than it would at £1m with B- or C-list stars. This is because the perception is that for a film to be promotable, it needs stars who will be interviewed on breakfast television sofas, in populist magazines like *Hello*, go on late night chat shows and, of course, walk down the red carpet at a glitzy West End première signing autographs and providing even more photo opportunities. *They* create the buzz.

This is why writing great roles that will challenge actors, bring out the best in them and transform their careers, giving them the chance of winning coveted awards, can be gold dust in your scripts. Television drama is every bit as star-led as the feature film world and, although the stars may differ, their value in getting a green light is much the same.

All of these things make up a snapshot of the issues involved in being a professional writer. In other words, you need to know more than how to write.

# 2 Research, training and networking

## Everything you need to know before you write your first script

## Research

If you are entirely new to writing for television, don't rush to put pen to paper. A year's gentle research into how the industry works will pay handsome dividends – and save you time in the long run.

Two very important things you can do are given below.

### 1. Read scripts

As a writer you will probably learn more from reading scripts than going to the movies or watching television. Few people will have read scripts while at school and even on a university degree course the number of scripts that are required reading is modest. For a serious writer one a day would be a good target, at least 300+ a year. Scripts are available freely on the web. The BBC writersroom website provides a range of BBC scripts but there are literally thousands of scripts available from dozens of websites. Be sure to get onto the writersroom newsletter mailing list and get regular updates from them.

> The BBC writersroom is a website (www.bbc.co.uk/writersroom) and a team of dedicated people who look for new, talented writers and help get their work to people within the BBC.

## 2. Read the 'trades'

Successful television writers will usually be regular readers of the television trade papers. In the UK the key publication is a weekly magazine called *Broadcast*. A subscription may appear expensive but it is invaluable for many reasons. Firstly, you will get an up-to-date analysis of what is happening in the television industry that could impact on your writing choices; secondly, by knowing what is happening you will be far more confident about being able to talk to producers about issues that affect them, even if they are not directly related to what you are writing. Producers like talking about themselves and if you are seen as someone who can join in a broad industry conversation and also, by being a clever writer, be a problem-solver, then producers will seek you.

> To ease the cost of a subscription to *Broadcast* magazine, why not share one with other writer friends, or find out whether your local library has it.

The trades are also a main source of knowing which companies are doing what, who has just moved jobs, what new series are being announced and what is happening in the ratings or box office. All of this is very important for your strategic planning.

Why do you need to know what others are doing in the industry? Very simple: you need to be able to talk to people about what is going up, what is going down, and what the future probably is, as far as you can see it. How else can you react to what they are wanting to do if you don't know what's happening?

Reading the trades is perhaps the most important preparation you can undertake as part of your submission strategy (apart from writing great spec scripts). www.twelvepoint.com used to publish

'The Buzz' – short items that were found in the trades. Below is an example of 'The Buzz' that will give you an idea of the sort of information available in the trades that are of interest to television writers.

Because many writers find the trade papers opaque and difficult to extract valuable information from, I have added comments about why these items of news are valuable to scriptwriters in italics. Information is gold dust, especially if you do not have an agent. Even if you do have an agent, it is a great way to keep them on their toes by pointing out the opportunities that they should be putting you up for.

These examples, which are not contemporary, demonstrate the richness of information that is available to you if you take a little trouble to examine the trades carefully.

- Ecosse Films are making an adaptation of Kate Atkinson's novel *Behind the Scenes at the Museum*, to be written by Brian Fillis (4 × 60'), Lucy Bedford Exec Produces for Kudos with Patrick Spence of BBC NI for the BBC. *[This item gives you two names for your potential submission list: Lucy Bedford and Patrick Spence. It is very important to collect the appropriate names at production companies and broadcasters.]*
- C4 Education boss Matt Locke is featured as The Commissioner *(Broadcast)*. The profile describes exactly what he is looking for. The channel is largely digital now. *[These profiles of commissioning editors are invaluable in that they tell you exactly what they are looking for, or at least what they say they are looking for!]*

- In Edinburgh (at the TV Festival) controller of Channel 5 Richard Woolf announced that the channel would not be able to commission original drama or comedy until after the recession *(Broadcast)*. *[OK, so cross C5 off your submission list for the moment.]*
- In a full-page in *Broadcast* about their Commissioning Index, we get more detail about the service (at http:// tci.broadcastnow.co.uk). The current database holds over 1,300 programmes, 170 commissioners and more than 170 indies in an interactive database. It gives production company statistics that enable you to understand the latest production and commissioning trends and gives you the ability to search by genre. It also gives the latest news on what is greenlit and who is who for every channel. *[Subscribers have access to this fabulous database of all television commissions, which is a brilliant way to find out who has commissioned or bought what. This kind of information can help you plan a careful and well-targeted submission strategy.]*

## Training

Training is not a one-stop solution but it can kick-start your career, especially if you use it to learn everything possible 'around' the focus of your subject. So a writer might study directing or acting to provide themselves with greater insight into the process by which films or television dramas are made, as opposed to studying genre theory, which in my opinion can be an academic, navel-gazing look at genre and has little to contribute to understanding why different audiences like different genres.

Working in a lowly position in a production company is likely to be as good for a writer's career as a degree in scriptwriting. Both would be ideal and, if your degree course does not make an internship part of the course, getting jobs during the holidays in a variety of production companies or literary agencies will definitely benefit your career. Make sure you meet as many industry contacts as possible during your degree or internship.

Don't assume that all scriptwriting degrees are equal, or that because a tutor has a few credits (even many) that they are a good teacher. Some of the best teachers are not writers and some good writers are not very good teachers.

There are many undergraduate and postgraduate screenwriting courses in the UK. The British Film Institute (BFI) website (www. bfi.org.uk) has a comprehensive list and Skillset is specifically about training (www.skillset.org). It is difficult to recommend specific courses since the teaching can be variable, as can the access to industry contacts provided by the course. For any given student, one course may be more effective than another. Do your research; speak to past students and current ones; ask contacts you may have in the industry. Your local (and convenient) institution may not necessarily be the best one for you.

That being said, the advantage of the better degree courses is that you will also meet and be mentored by leading industry players. When deciding on which university or film school to go to – if that is what you decide to do – check out how many industry visitors you will have every year and their calibre. It makes a difference.

Your choice of formal training therefore depends on a number of factors as follows.

1. If you are passionate about film or television then there are good degree courses available, but beware of courses that are very academic and seem to regard the 'industry' as something a little distasteful. Most people we have met who want to be writers want to work in the industry rather than get degrees. It is a vocation and the best training is usually that which takes this into account.

2. Consider an undergraduate degree in psychology (good for understanding how and why characters behave the way they do) or law (always useful for getting work in the industry) before going on to a postgraduate degree in scriptwriting like the one Chris Walker, John Cooke and I set up at De Montfort.

3. There are numerous short courses in all aspects of writing and many writers use this as a way of getting the latest thinking. These courses are run by film schools and universities as well as organisations such as the London Screenwriters' Festival (www.londonscreenwritersfestival.com) and Euroscript (www. euroscript.co.uk).

> Talk to other writers about their courses: did they find them useful, what were the tutors like, were good industry contacts made there?

Finally, there are dozens of books on scriptwriting and while it is useful to test your own attitudes and knowledge out by reading books on how to write, be careful of following them (or the courses) slavishly because it can lead to writing-by-numbers (this is equally true of this book as any other!). More information is provided later in the book and in the 'Resources' section on page 271. Finally the BBC Writers Academy is worth a look if you have some credits.

---

### BBC Writers Academy

Launched in 2005, the BBC Writers Academy works as an apprenticeship for writers. The first part involves a three-month course led by John Yorke, Controller of Drama. Writers then complete a broadcast episode of *Doctors*, and if this is accepted they then complete commissions on *Casualty, Holby* and *EastEnders*.

Eight writers are selected out of hundreds of applicants to undergo the intensive 15-month programme designed to equip them with all the skills necessary to write successfully for BBC drama. The course entails classroom training, lectures from the country's best writers, instruction in all aspects of television production, and direct writing experience on the four continuing drama shows.

---

## Networking

You may think that this comes after having a submission strategy but it should not. Agents and producers go to events of all sorts. We attend film and television festivals and markets, awards and screening ceremonies, and parties given by the companies and organisations in the industry. It is always easier to talk to someone when you are meeting in a neutral place. These meetings are key to developing a submission strategy since people tell you what they are looking for (you may have to ask!).

Set up a writers' group if you can't find one and join the Writers' Guild and the London Screenwriters' Festival network. Don't think they are an unnecessary expense or that you don't really need to belong to them. You do. The Guild has student and candidate membership and the festival is a must-attend event with much going on outside the festival itself. The internet is an easy place to network. Write in to independent filmmakers network Shooting People, join chat groups and forums. Writers share information even though they are in competition. Be generous with information and you will receive more back.

If you meet an agent at a networking event or reception or screening, it is easy to ask if they are looking for clients or – better – what kind of clients they are looking for. If you fit the bill then pitch yourself, starting with your track record and credits. If you have none it is more difficult, which is why it is important to get credits, hence why working on soaps or series is so valuable because it is the easiest way to get credits. See Chapter 9 for more on getting an agent.

The kinds of questions you can ask an agent at a gathering include whether they are looking to take on new clients, and in what areas of writing (they may want stage play writers or film writers not television writers, or the other way round). You can ask producers what they are currently working on (I ask this frequently); whether they are currently looking for writers or projects. If you read the trades and are up to speed on the most recent news in the industry, there will always be items to chat about. The effect of BBC budget cutbacks has been a running question for the last year or so and will be for several years to come!

Once you have got a feel for the industry you will be in a much stronger position to put together the portfolio of sparkling calling card or 'spec' scripts that will be your key tool in breaking in. Now it is time to start writing in earnest!

# 3 Calling card scripts

How to put together a balanced portfolio
of spec scripts, and how to use peer-review
and script-reading services to best effect

## What kind of scripts should I write?

Spec scripts are the main way you convince other people in the industry that you can write. You need to have a portfolio of original scripts that demonstrate your versatility. It should contain scripts of the standard television slot lengths (30, 60, 90 minutes plus a feature film-length single of say a maximum of 110 minutes).

There should be examples of different genres and formats (such as comedy, thriller, domestic drama, soap, perhaps children's content). A BBC (or public service broadcast) 60-minute slot will need a script of up to 57 minutes; on commercial television, a 60-minute slot needs a script of up to 52 minutes (as well as having the drama structured around the ad breaks).

The portfolio also needs some very original writing that does not 'fit' the existing shows, because many producers believe that when a writer does something 'original' it reveals qualities that enable the producer to select more appropriately.

However, there is some risk involved in assuming that 'original' means something that has never been done or that is wacky and wild. 'Original' means that the writer has contributed to all aspects of the script, from the idea and the structure of the story to the characters and dialogue.

To some extent it is a good way to evaluate the judgement of a writer: do they understand genre (and have they understood the important genre conventions)? Can they write dialogue that adds to rather than mirrors the action? Do the characters engage the reader emotionally? All these are important to get right.

What is also difficult for writers at the beginning of their careers is judging what they are best at. Try to focus on your strengths (which may not be what you happen to most like watching).

> One of the best calling cards I have ever seen (I took on the writer on the strength of it) was an *AbFab* script. It was so good that it very nearly got her work on the show. I would recommend that at least one of your calling cards is based on an existing show since it provides evidence of your ability to work with other people's characters and storylines.

Basically there are three main formats or slot lengths for calling card scripts: 30, 60 and 90 minutes. The 30-minute script could be a soap episode written on spec or a sitcom.

Your 50- or 60-minute drama scripts can also be derivative or based on an existing show but I would recommend that you also write something original. These days a deal for an original $2 \times 50$ or $3 \times 50$ is possible for a relatively new writer so it is worth showing that you can hold the tension for at least 50 minutes.

Your 90-minute script is like a film, usually a single, though there have also been 2 × 90 or 3 × 90-minute miniseries. Here you must do something original and preferably so tight, so neatly structured according to classical movie structure, that anyone reading the script knows that you know what you are doing.

It is not possible to predict exactly what people reading samples are mostly affected by, except that demonstrating that you have judgement and know how to make audiences laugh and cry will usually succeed.

I would not use an adaptation of a novel as a calling card (unless you are applying for a job adapting a novel) mainly because you must have permission to do the adaptation from the novelist, and you cannot sell your script unless the rights to the novel are available to be sold. If you own those rights, you can then make that deal. So an out-of-copyright novel might be a better bet.

Whenever you write an original calling card script, you should always write with the intention of selling, so make it appeal to some identifiable part of the market.

> A client of mine wrote a perfectly structured thriller that was very lean and focused on three central characters. It attracted a director who admired the work but was unable to buy it. A little later the director was asked to become involved in an unwritten miniseries and he recommended my client for the job.

## How do I make sure my scripts are the best they can possibly be?

Don't send out a first- or even second-draft script as a calling card! You only get one chance to impress, so rewrite and polish until your scripts sparkle.

Ideally, the first step for your script is to subject it to a rigorous peer-review: you should have a few friends who are writers and you should all read each other's treatments and scripts. There are various ways of approaching this, from setting up a writers' group to Adrian Mead's 'Power of 3' method: www.meadkerr.com/making-it-as-a-screen-writer.

When you peer-review, you should each aim to be constructively critical, by which I mean that if you have a criticism, it should be accompanied by a constructive suggestion or solution. Do note, you are not meant to be rewriting the script, only putting forward ideas for the writer of the script to consider and make their own.

Having given each other notes, each of you should rewrite, get more feedback and rewrite again. Once you've been through this process you might consider paying for a professional script report. These can cost anything from £50 to £500 per script, depending on the experience of the reader – so you don't want to waste your money by sending them a first draft! Use peer-review first. And do some quick research before you send any money for a script report. Ideally, only use a service where you have a first-hand recommendation. As with any unlicensed trade, there are some excellent professional script readers out there … and some less excellent ones. Among the better-known UK organisations and individuals offering this service are: Bang2Write, Kate Leys, The Script Factory, Industrial Scripts and ScriptAngel.

Then, having considered all the notes you've received, rewrite it again, making sure it is as good as you can possibly make it. Don't follow notes blindly and don't write anything you really don't believe in. If you can get a group of actors to do a reading (aloud) you will learn a great deal about your script, particularly its weak spots. This will help you improve it further when you rewrite.

Without really good and polished calling card scripts, you will not give those in the industry the chance to discover you. If you remember that spec scripts are rarely sold, then you will realise that you will end up with a number of unsold calling card scripts during your career, but the really good ones will have got you work. Experienced writers often have several such scripts in their bottom drawer.

Once you have a set of scripts you're happy with, it's time to start thinking about sending them out.

# 4 Submission strategies

Where to send your work, and how to present it to give you the best chance of success

## Structure of the television industry in the UK

Some knowledge of the structure of the television industry is essential to kick-start your career, or to develop it in new directions if you already have a career. For a relative beginner, with no credits or commissions, it is important to get to know the 'players' who can help you get into the industry – or move around in it – from agents to script editors, from producers to directors and, perhaps most easily accessible and helpful, other writers. For those who already have a foot on the ladder, for example, a soap writer who may want to move away from 30-minute slots into hour-long slots, this means having longer calling card scripts and getting to know a different group of script editors and producers.

As discussed in the previous chapter, a useful strategy is to have a selection of calling card scripts that demonstrate your ability and talent and your range. By also having an understanding of the structure of the television industry, including some detailed knowledge of which broadcasters or production companies you intend to submit to, you will have some targets: what kinds of scripts to write and where you intend to submit them.

This chapter explains how to use the structure of the industry to help you develop that all-important submission strategy: whom to submit to and what to submit.

## Who will read your script?

The simplest picture of the television industry is a hierarchy as follows.

- Broadcasters.
- Large independent production companies.
- Small independent production companies.
- Tiny independent production companies (often a one-person company though that person might be experienced).
- Script editors or development producers.
- Agents.
- Script readers.
- Established writers.
- Beginner writers.

The broadcasters decide what gets shown; they buy most programmes (that they do not produce themselves) from the large independent production companies; they buy fewer from small independent companies and less from tiny (one person) companies.

Breaking in is therefore like climbing a mountain: the broadcasters at the top and perhaps you at – or near – the bottom. You should always be thinking about whom to submit to, especially before you write a script. You ought to have several companies or producers in mind and, in order to do this effectively, you need to know who the better independent production companies are and what they produce. You should also know what the various broadcasters tend to broadcast in the genres and formats in which you want to write. Or choose to write what you know they want.

There are several ways of finding out who the best companies are for what you want to write.

1. Read the trade press or 'trades' as discussed in Chapter 1.

2. Research organisations like the Producers' Alliance for Cinema and Television (PACT) who have a website which provides information on independent production companies.

3. Talk to other writers.

4. Network at events like The London Screenwriters' Festival. Delegates get access to most of the filmed sessions and interviews with many well-known writers and producers even if they cannot attend the festival or all of the sessions (there are far more sessions than any one person can attend).

5. Do a degree at a film school or university that has a large number of industry lecturers.

6. Use other sources, such as the BBC writersroom or *Broadcast* magazine (a weekly publication) for the data on which shows are doing well. From this information you can tell which companies have produced the shows that use scripted drama or comedy and which shows were produced in-house by broadcasters. By checking the websites of production companies you will find out if they accept scripts from unagented writers. Many do not and there is no easy way round this. Getting an agent (see later) is the most effective way, but persevering, meeting producers at events

and festivals and seminars is perhaps next best. There are also many articles in www.twelvepoint.com by John Peek or Paul Youngbluth of TAPE that are about how the television industry works, both here and in the USA.

7. Watch shows and make a note of the names of the script editors listed in the credits. If you think your best calling card script will appeal to a similar audience as the show you have seen, submit to the script editor named in the credits and go online to find the email address of the company in question or call their switchboard.

Of the 10 TV shows that received the highest ratings in 2010, only four were scripted dramas or soaps, the rest being reality shows or sporting events. In other words, not very much television is scripted and this gives you an insight into the apparently closed shop: not many slots are available and there are many experienced writers out there aiming for those slots.

This should focus your attention on what you need to know, and what material you need to prepare in order to attract the attention of the 'gatekeepers' in the industry, the people who can help you move your career forward (or hinder you). Knowing what shows use writers and also understanding how the 'A-list' writers who penned them got to where they are, will give you valuable information about how you should plan your career.

*Doctor Who, EastEnders, Downton Abbey* and *Coronation Street* were the four scripted shows that made the Top 10 in 2010. None of these are shows first-time writers can get onto. *Doctor Who* and *Downton Abbey* are shows that only the top writers tend to write; these shows are accessible only once you start getting some credits.

There are shows such as *Hollyoaks* and *Doctors* which are considered easier-access shows for relative beginners; but *EastEnders* and *Coronation Street* (as well as *Holby* and *Casualty*) are hard to get onto unless you have something of a track record that demonstrates that you can and have delivered scripts on time and satisfactorily to several production companies (or even to one company if you have done several episodes).

This is partly because all the soaps have tight delivery deadlines for episodes: each episode will have a transmission date and risking an episode on a writer who may need so many rewrites that the episode might miss that date is simply not a risk the broadcasters will take.

So establishing your credits or track record is critically important because it is proof that you can deliver scripts on time. Sadly, sometimes the credits do not bring in much money, but in the long term, credits will help a writer get more work and lead to deals that do pay better.

---

### Formats and genres

It is important to not confuse the words 'format' and 'genre'. In television a format refers to the length of the show or the kind of show: formats include sitcom (30-minute slot), soap (also 30-minute slot), drama (usually 60-minute slot), quiz show, makeover show, movie and so on.

A genre refers to conventions that enable audiences to connect with shows (and genres are also usually written with a capital letter): Thrillers, Mysteries, Romances,

---

Comedy and so on. There are some terms that are less clear: Western is not strictly a genre but a location, as is Sci-Fi. You can have almost all the genres in those two locations. But this is a fairly academic split hair and ordinary audiences will refer to these terms as if they were genres. See more in Part Two on both of these.

## The broadcasters

The conventional wisdom is that – with the exception of the BBC writersroom, or any competitions run by the broadcasters – there is not much point in beginner writers submitting directly to the main broadcasters: the BBC, ITV, Channel 4, Sky and Channel 5. Sky does big brand-name drama almost always written by very experienced writers sometimes called 'showrunners'.

A showrunner is effectively a writer who produces the show; he or she may also be called the 'head' writer. They will select the other writers and often polish the scripts by those writers as well as writing a number of episodes themselves.

Currently, Steven Moffat is the showrunner for *Doctor Who*. If you want to write for this show and have no credits the chances are probably nil of a spec *Doctor Who* script you submit even being read. This is for legal reasons: the show does not wish to risk the possibility that if you and one of their writers had similar ideas you could attempt to sue them. However much you love *Doctor Who*, earn your dues first and get a fair number of credits on other shows before expecting to be taken seriously by a showrunner.

Channel 5 does not produce any original drama at the time of writing this book. Channel 4 buys its drama from independent producers and ITV largely does so too. So it is more sensible to target independent producers; and the way in to many of them is through their development executives or script editors.

## Script editors

At most production companies, except perhaps the smallest, there is a person primarily responsible for finding new writers and new projects, and working with the writers who are hired. They are called 'script editors' or 'development executives'. The smaller companies don't always have a script editor on staff, but hire one in for each project they produce, so there you may be dealing directly with the producer.

As well as submitting your material to them, script editors are also a primary target for networking, as are development executives and producers. Use every opportunity to get to know them personally, at whatever networking gatherings you can attend. Many of them will agree to read a script you ask to submit. The personal touch at events is disproportionately valuable and at events like the London Screenwriters' Festival you can see the focused writers meeting people rather than going to the sessions.

Always try to prioritise local or regional producers in your area. Don't assume that London is where everything happens; it is not, and if you don't live in or near London the chances are probably greater if you focus on producers who are local to you.

But living in Wales, where *Doctor Who* is produced, or Birmingham, where *Doctors* is produced, won't necessarily help, except you might find it easier to meet staff from those shows at local events or workshops.

The script editor's job should be to help the writer realise the best script they can, that serves the needs of the production company or broadcaster. There is obviously room here for a conflict of interests: when the writer and the company disagree on the direction of the script, the script editor, while championing the writer, has nevertheless to deliver a script that the bosses (whether broadcaster or independent producer) want.

Good script editors are amazing diplomats (or as one writer once said to me, they are amazingly two-faced). They can be your most important ally (apart from your agent if you have one), so nurture the relationship. A script editor progresses their career by finding and getting great work out of writers: remember they need you as much as you need them, so try to be an asset.

There are also 'script readers' who work under script editors. Often the script editor is also the reader in a company; especially in the smaller ones. The reader's job is to recommend suitable projects for the company. These are some of the things to try and avoid, as a reader is unlikely to recommend any of the following.

1. A badly-written script.

2. A genre that the company does not want.

3. A genre that they already have projects in (so do not want more of).

4. A format that they do not want (e.g. a long-running series when they want singles or two-parters; or a sitcom when they don't produce sitcoms).

5. An ambitious project, perhaps many episodes, from a writer who has no track record at all and therefore has not proved that they can write on time and to budget and can take notes, though if the writing is good it might serve as a calling card script and get you hired to do something else which the company is already doing.

6. Arrogant and over-the-top covering letters demonstrating the amateurishness of the writer.

So, there are many obstacles, but understanding the responsibilities of the people you will be dealing with should help eliminate some of these obstacles.

> If you have a track record, it may be more appropriate to approach the producer, who is more senior than the script editor. But do not go behind the back of the script editor. Make an ally.

Treat the layer of script readers and editors between you and the producers as potential champions of your work. They will often reject you (so get used to it!) but they are the gatekeepers you need to get past. Their career development actually depends not on who they reject but on what talent they discover. They can therefore help filter your material, providing you with valuable feedback to improve your script before it goes to producers or broadcasters who might pay you for it.

## Producers

Producers are either 'independent' or work for broadcasters. You can approach either although generally smaller independent producers are more likely to work with newer writers. Independent producers are often called 'indies'. Concentrate on producers you know something about, preferably when you have met someone or have a recommendation. However, by being able to identify heads of drama or comedy, you can more easily approach them in a social or networking setting using their first name even if this is cheeky. If emailing, say Dear Bill (never Dear Sir), after all, they are unlikely to remember if they have met you or not.

It is usually best to concentrate on local producers, development being a messy and face-to-face business. Working at great distances (such as UK to Los Angeles) is difficult and relatively rare.

## Going global

What about Hollywood or HBO or the American networks? Forget them for the time being. Once you have become a hit in your own country, then worry about Hollywood *et al.*

The same is not true about Germany, however, as they do use some non-German language writers. If you can write a tightly-structured genre Thriller or Comedy or Romantic Comedy (which means having a calling card that proves it or an agent who is trusted by the producers) then you might get a German television movie deal. They can pay £1,000–£1,500 for the treatment and option, and up to £30,000 for the script, which is not bad for a movie that no one you know is likely to see. It is not easy. The standards are high and there is a good deal of competition but it is one of the many ways you can focus your research and attention. Meeting German producers in Cannes or at the Berlinale can help you get your work read. Some of them attend the London Screenwriters' Festival.

Treat going to Cannes or Berlin like a working holiday: being there means you will meet producers and the fact that you are there will make them take you more seriously than they might otherwise. See films, talk to industry people at as many parties as you can crash. Learn about the business. Every day there is at least one daily trade paper. Get it first thing in the morning and read it carefully cover to cover. Note announcements about production companies producing shows or films that are similar to what you write best. Try to meet them socially and use your social skills (a bit of flattery never hurts!). It might turn out to be a rather good holiday. Be passionate about the industry you want to work in; many of the people you will meet are passionate about it and therefore you already have something in common. But don't go in being very ignorant about the business because you will not impress.

If you are invited to a face-to-face meeting (because you submitted a script which a producer or script editor has read and liked or because you meet at a gathering), you will need to pitch your project or projects. A pitch is a short verbal proposal. It may take one or two minutes to recite (and be based on a single written paragraph). There is a shorter version called 'the elevator pitch' (because it is so short that you could do it in an elevator when travelling down a few floors with a producer).

Prepare for your verbal pitch by writing a succinct, one-paragraph description of your work. The classic advice is to state whose story it is, what it is they want and what or who is stopping them getting it. Obviously this doesn't apply to every possible story but you should see the principle.

Knowing your one paragraph well will make you sound more confident. Make strong eye contact. Be enthusiastic and *never* read it from a piece of paper.

## What are they looking for?

Producers, script readers and editors know what their bosses and the broadcasters are looking for. Being courteous and businesslike and getting a chance to meet one of them (usually only after they have read and liked a script) gives you the opportunity to find out more about what they are seeking.

After over 25 years in the business I treat almost every meeting with a producer or script editor as an opportunity to ask what they are looking for. And it changes from month to month. So you need to be constantly updating your knowledge.

Understanding the tastes and needs of broadcasters is essential if you want to write for television and are serious about actually earning a living. Experienced writers have had a range of experiences from which they have learned a great deal and they have usually watched a lot of television.

If television drama is what you want to write, you need to watch as much that is made domestically as possible, recording it, deconstructing some of the episodes (watch recordings more than once and write down how many scenes there are and how the act breaks fall so that you begin to see the hidden skeleton of the structure until this becomes second nature). Experienced writers will also usually look at who produced, directed and script-edited a particular show or episode and note those names that impressed them, these being the people you want to try to meet.

You should also watch international drama, especially the best of American television drama, and note the differences. See what you can learn from it but bear in mind the very different structure of the television industry: in North America commissions for a series are usually 22 or more episodes as opposed to the European commission of six or seven in the first instance.

So the key thing in breaking in is to know what to write for whom. Different producers look for different genres and formats, usually depending on what the broadcasters say they want. However, you cannot rely on public statements even if they are made in *Broadcast* magazine. The truth is that the needs of broadcasters constantly change; this is why having friends among the script editors who can tell you the latest before it becomes public is invaluable.

One week a broadcaster says they do not want male-oriented cop shows because there are too many; the next week they commission another, perhaps because something particularly good is offered to them, usually by a showrunner writer. This is frustrating for other writers who had similar ideas that were not picked up.

The problem is that producers and broadcasters need to be confident in the writer as well as in the idea. This is why proving yourself is so important early on in your career. Patience is also important because once you have developed a script and polished it and find out that a similar show is about to be broadcast, all you can do is put it away for a couple of years and swiftly develop something else.

Television is even more difficult to break into now than it was five or 10 years ago. Would Julian Fellowes have had the lavish *Downton Abbey* commissioned if he had not previously won an Oscar? (It reportedly cost £1m per episode to produce.) Probably not, even though he has many other credits going back to 1975, including TV series like *Heartbeat* and *Monarch of the Glen* (check them out on the IMDb website: www.imdb.com).

So, short of winning an Oscar (or other respectable credits) first, writers need to be focused, determined and single-minded when it comes to making the breakthrough into the world of writing for television.

It is difficult but not that difficult if the right choices are made and there is appropriate preparation. By making self-indulgent choices, the odds of breaking through are considerably narrowed.

Of course, it is not only a question of researching the most appropriate shows for yourself to target. Understanding what makes great writing affect the audience is also important. Provoking emotion in audiences and having the techniques to do that (which are explained later in the book) is possibly the most important quality of a successful scriptwriter and is also necessary to make that breakthrough. In some respects it may be even more important in that if your scripts do evoke emotion in those who read them, they will want to work with you even if you have little idea about what it is you should be writing.

Soaps and series like *EastEnders* and *Coronation Street* are the real training ground, for television writers. Most of the leading 'show-runners' (including Jimmy McGovern, Tony Jordan, Matthew Graham, and Ashley Pharoah) cut their teeth writing soaps. Check out their CVs on the web to see how they spent their first few years as writers.

### How many projects does the company have on their 'slate'?

It is sometimes better to work with a good smaller or medium-sized company (one that has a couple of high-profile shows broadcast) who may have less funding but also fewer projects in development. Many writers suffer in development hell because they work with large companies who develop many projects but only make a few. And if you do have to do dozens of rewrites, it is less painful if your script is actually produced.

On the other hand, the bigger and better financed a company, the more likely it is to have the muscle to keep your project going when the going gets tough. Having a close, trusting and open relationship is probably more important than just the size of the production company. For submitting to agents see Chapter 9.

## How are television shows developed?

Many television programmes start as an idea in the mind of the producer. They may work for a broadcaster, be a freelancer for an independent production company, or be employed by a major production company (they may even own the company!).

There are numerous companies that all generate a vast number of ideas, which they pitch to commissioning editors who work for the broadcasters to 'buy' or commission. Usually a commission occurs before all the development work, including scripts, has been completed. On a commission the broadcaster will usually put up some or all of the money to enable the script/s to be written (or rewritten if one already exists).

So the writer working alone and pitching ideas is competing with the producers (who are on an inside track) to come up with new concepts in which the broadcaster will invest money. To compete successfully you often need to be original or come up with a new and strong way of doing something, *and* have a magnificent calling card script. You need to demonstrate industry knowledge and talent in equal proportions in order to be picked up by producers and broadcasters.

> Broadcasters will often not fully finance a programme or show. Some of the bigger, independent producers will invest some of the budget from their own financial resources, which also makes them and the show they are proposing more attractive to the broadcaster.

One of the reasons for writing a number of great calling card scripts is that you send these to many producers and if they like the writing they will take note of you. It is unlikely they will buy the script unless it fits into a programme slot that they know has space for more material. What is more likely is that they will contact you when they have a bite from a broadcaster for an idea (or they are optimistic they will get a bite) and they remember that they liked your script in a similar genre. Many writers get their first paid commissions that way.

In other words, you often earn money writing not what you want to write, but what a producer who is paying you wants you to write. You are a 'writer for hire'. If you are able to approach every meeting with a prospective paymaster with this in mind, you will be flexible and open-minded and are more likely to have people wanting to work with you.

So shows are developed because broadcasters put out a call for something particular, because producers do the same (whether or not they know what the broadcaster actually wants); or because both of them come across some wonderful material or idea from a writer who has proved in the past that they can deliver.

Where does that leave the beginner writer with a great idea? Well, firstly, can they be sure that it is a great idea? Many pitches include the words 'This has never been done before . . .' and when one looks at it, it becomes clear why it has never been done before. But there are instances of relatively new writers developing cracking ideas, supported by beautifully written spec scripts. So it can be done. But generally a more predictable career path is entering and winning some scriptwriting competitions, writing some great shorts which are produced, then getting some television credits for easier-access shows before your original idea is picked up.

## Knowing how to catch the editor's eye

Good writing will win out. Good ideas are relatively easy to come across; it is good execution that is difficult to find. So what you think is a good idea may not carry as much weight in a submission as how well it is written. A not very good idea, wonderfully written, will usually attract attention and get you a meeting. So don't rely on the idea to carry you through. In addition, going to the market too early – before an original script is ready and fully polished – will probably result in a rejection. So get objective eyes – be it via your writer's group, your agent or lecturers – to advise you as to whether your script is ready.

Remember that you are trying to break into an industry, and that you are writing for others rather than for yourself. There is nothing wrong with 'self-indulgent' writing if that is what you want to do. But don't expect others to value your work as highly as you do, unless you are very talented and you manage to write in formats and genres that they are looking for.

## Competitions

There are all sorts of competitions, many for shorts. Go for them. Submit scripts for readings to organisations like Rocliffe or The Script Factory. If you are selected, it gives you and your script great exposure. At the very least you should make sure you are on their mailing lists.

They can also provide script analysis as well as the readings and Euroscript also organises training courses, see www.euroscript.com.

Rocliffe Forum does rehearsed readings in front of industry pros and has just organised its first reading in New York! Visit www.rocliffe.com.

Some broadcasters have initiatives and there are also prizes like the Tony Jordan/Danny Stack Red Planet prize (www.redplanetpictures.co.uk/prize.php). This is organised with leading indie Kudos Film and Television. The prize started in 2007 with the objective of nurturing aspiring writers and finding new writing talent. The judging panels include the great and good from British television. This is a competition definitely worth entering.

The London Screenwriters' Festival initiated a £5,000 prize with the Wellcome Foundation for a one-page treatment of an idea for the screen inspired by science (www.londonscreenwritersfestival.com; www.wellcome.ac.uk).

It is worth researching the many competitions that exist and being quite promiscuous about entering them. Check the BBC writersroom, amongst other places, for screenwriting competitions.

## Submission packages

Once you have created a list of producers and editors and agents you are going to target you should send them your submission, which should include all of the following.

- A covering letter or email (my advice is that – unless it has been made clear that a hard copy submission is specifically required – you should submit electronically and state in your email that if they prefer a hard copy, they should let you know and you will send one).
- Your CV.
- A treatment describing the proposed show.
- A full script, either for the programme in question or one of your strongest, most relevant, original calling card scripts (and make sure the pages are numbered!). Don't put a © line on every page. This makes you look paranoid. See page 58 for a brief overview of copyright.
- Return postage (if you did not email the submission).

### The covering letter

The letter should be concise. Make sure you do the following.

- Give a little information about yourself, especially if you have been nominated for or won any awards or competitions.
- Explain why you have written what you are submitting.

- Explain whether you have been optioned (see Chapter 7 for more on this), commissioned or produced before.
- State how long the script is.
- State what the market is for the script as you see it ('I understand that your company is looking for a post-watershed sitcom.' Or 'I believe BBC1 is looking for something along the lines of the drama series I have developed.')
- Mention what you know about what they produce (or if submitting to an agent, what kind of writer they represent) and why that attracts you to them. This can be difficult as an agent might not actually want writers who are very similar to those they already represent; they may perhaps prefer a writer offering something different. But, for example, an agent who may represent teenage drama may not want a writer offering material aimed at 3 to 5 year olds.

Make sure you don't do any of the following.

- Oversell. I often reject people because they have totally unrealistic ideas of their worth and of the market. It is just too much hard work teaching them everything, unless the script is magic, which it rarely is.
- Mention that you have submitted to other agents (even if you have).

### The CV: building your track record and credits

If your CV has no scriptwriting credits, make sure that it does contain something relevant. Any other writing credits will count; training will count; if you have won any writing prizes, even for short stories or journalism, then mention them.

If you have acted, directed, read scripts professionally (i.e. been paid a few pounds) or done anything relevant, emphasise it. Students of the BA in Scriptwriting at Bournemouth University, who have to complete six weeks of work experience, make more mileage out of that in many cases than they do out of a term's work.

If you have any credits, shout them from the rooftops: shorts produced, nominations in competitions, stage plays at little, unheard-of theatres, sketches, anything.

A student from the BA at Bournemouth wrote articles on spec for *ScriptWriter*, which I published. He used them to get a job as a script reader because his CV looked stronger. He then found a place on an MA in creative writing. On graduating he found a job with a media company. He applied for *Hollyoaks* (sending copies of his articles with his calling card script) and was given his first television commission. He did several episodes, sold a radio play and was in a better position to apply for a wider range of scriptwriting work.

Some of you are no doubt not too keen on writing for soaps, but they are the real testing-ground. Some of you may want to write sitcoms. Well, I'm afraid there are virtually no sitcom slots for unproduced writers, but sketch-writing and stand-up comedy could be a good training ground. Graham Linehan and Arthur Matthews of *Father Ted* fame started by writing short sketches for programmes like the *Fast Show*. In all cases, you have to be apprenticed for a while to prove you can deliver good work on time and unfortunately apprentices usually have little say about what they do while being apprenticed.

So, don't focus all your attention on writing only original material. Identify shows that other people have created, shows that need writers, however difficult it is to get onto them. Decide which of your lovingly-prepared calling card scripts is most appropriate, for example, a spec comedy feature film script that demonstrates how well you write comedy is fine to submit for a television comedy writing opportunity or perhaps even for a soap but not for a dark crime drama series.

## Written pitches or selling documents

I would like to suggest a very effective way of writing documents that will help you sell yourself and your ideas. This approach breaks the document down into four parts. We evolved this method of writing selling documents (which are sometimes called treatments) over years of noting what it was that most producers and publishers reacted well to.

The reality is that everyone seems to want the information in a different order, and a single, monolithic document that contains *all* the information you need to provide will be confusing to read. This stems from the fact that you may have spent weeks or months thinking about the plot, developing back-stories for the characters and so on, but a document of a few pages, unless broken into appropriate headings, will be difficult to read.

So what are the appropriate headings for your selling document?

1. The blurb (half a page, written like the text on the back cover of a paperback best-seller, telling the reader what kind of story it is rather than telling them the story).

2. CVs of characters (five to 10 lines for a major character, three for a minor character; two pages in all, max).

3. A statement of intent (why you are writing this and why it is the right subject for you, less than a page).

4. The synopsis written in the present tense. This can be two to three pages; imagine you put the DVD on and describe the film or drama by concentrating on the visual aspects of the story. The present tense creates greater immediacy, the visual aspect making it easier to 'see'.

## What if I don't hear anything?

Politely enquire via the agent or producer's assistant after six weeks. Then try again after another six weeks. If this seems very slow remember that they might receive thousands of submissions and going through them is not really their highest priority. I think it is perfectly reasonable to submit to more than one person at a time (though not everyone agrees with me). I suggest that you either state up front that you are sending this to 'a couple of other people at the same time', or just don't say anything. The worst that can happen (apart from everyone rejecting you) is that two will want your material. If they took a long time you can say you had assumed that their silence was taken as a rejection. But that is quite a pleasant problem to have to deal with.

# 5 What happens next?

## How to deal with rejection – and what to do when you get an offer

### Rejection

There is a variation of an old joke in which a writer is at the reception desk of a television company. The receptionist says 'The Commissioning Editor for Drama isn't in but I will reject your script if you like!'

This tells us three things: getting commissioned is difficult; you shouldn't try to personally see the person to whom you have submitted material; and the person who rejects your work might well be unqualified to do so, but they still have the power to do it!

You must not take rejection letters too seriously or literally. One problem in trying to deduce much from a rejection letter may be due to the fact that the person who has read it doesn't have time or even good reasons for rejecting it but has to say something and that something is usually bland and unhelpful. However, if two or more people say the same thing, then it is probably correct (especially if it is critical of your work).

Agents find it easier to accept rejection because it is not their work, though it is their judgement that is being rejected.

If you receive a number of rejections, perhaps you should stop submitting the script without doing more work on it as your reputation might be affected. Companies usually keep records of what has been submitted by whom, so it is best to try a new piece of work.

No one likes to be rejected yet rejection is an inevitable experience in the business. You need to build up your confidence so that it doesn't put you off your stride.

If it helps, remember that almost every successful writer has had many rejections! An iconic BBC TV series, *Our Friends in the North*, written by the distinguished Peter Flannery and produced by the equally distinguished Michael Wearing and Charles Pattinson, took nine years in development before finally being transmitted.

## Getting offers

If your submission receives a positive reaction, know how to react. Do not seem to be overly grateful or rush into signing anything (even if you are ecstatic!). The contract will almost certainly give the producer all sorts of control over you and your work which are not easy to accept, including the right of cut-off (i.e. the right to fire you), so you need to retain some power during the contract negotiations. You should know what kind of changes they have in mind before you sell to them. This may sound obvious but most writers don't seem to think about it during contract negotiations.

When you receive an offer or a producer says he or she wants to buy your script (or commission you to write something), if possible, avoid naming your price (except to say that you are usually paid

Writers' Guild minimums or over). But you should know how prices are calculated. The Guild has established minimum fees below which writers try not to accept deals. This is not always possible because sometimes producers really do not have the money available to pay out, but it is worth trying to achieve it even if you are a beginner. See subsequent chapters on negotiating contracts for more detail.

Know the Writers' Guild minimums off by heart and always fix your price as a percentage of the budget. Even if the budget isn't known at this moment – which it won't be – then pegging your ultimate fee as a percentage of the budget is the safest way of ensuring an appropriate fee (see Chapter 7 for more details on this).

Be prepared to say no (either as a strategy or with finality) if the offer is not a good one. It gives you real power.

Understand the limitations of writing without pay and know how to improve your deal if you are deferring (or investing in the production).

What this means is that if you defer some of your payment, which is due at a later stage, you are, in effect, investing in the development. Like any investor, you should be recompensed in some way which should be itemised in the contract, perhaps with a bonus when the film goes into production. For example, if it is your idea, there should be a clause in the contract stating that they cannot fire you until you have been paid at least the usual first draft script delivery amount and that you should receive some more money on the first day of principal photography even if you have been fired and another writer hired.

If a producer says that they want a free option because they have no money themselves but they will work really hard to raise the money to make the film, say that if they do not want to pay for an option, it can't be a very high priority for them. If you don't put a value and a price on your work and talent, then why should anyone else?

Furthermore, if you defer, you should have some of the benefits of an investor, not only what writers are usually paid. You could be a co-producer or associate producer, and your percentage of the profits should be higher.

## Establishing yourself

Once you have kick-started a track record, you need to start submitting different kinds of work, so you need a different strategy. Firstly, if you are working reasonably regularly for a series or two, you will be meeting script editors regularly. They and the producers for whom they work will move to other series or shows, and if they have liked working with you, and rate your writing, they may well invite you to write for them on their new show.

The important strategy is to move to longer formats – there is a recognised career progression for writers from 30 minutes to 60 and then to 90 minutes. Apart from the pay being better, it is generally considered to be more demanding and the right direction for a career. A lead writer for *EastEnders* makes around £7,000 per episode and will probably be on the writing staff, i.e. doing a set number of episodes each year. *The Bill* used to pay £8,000–£12,000 for someone relatively new, and someone experienced received over £13,000. For *Spooks* it was £12,000–£18,000 an episode but they only took experienced writers. There are also repeat fees for most soap and series episodes.

Once you have your foot in the door of the industry, you will need to work just as hard to keep it there. As you start getting regular work, you will be presented with a range of different types of contract. The following chapters provide more detail on offers, options, contracts and negotiating tactics.

# Part Two
# Making a living

Part Two
Making Medicine

# 6 Negotiating writers' contracts

## The different types of writer's contract, and why you need to understand them

One of the ways you will be labelled a novice (meaning a producer or script editor won't invest significant time reading your script or listening to your pitch) is by demonstrating naïveté or ignorance about the business aspects of the career you have chosen. For example, asking a producer or script editor (or whoever speaks to you about a possible commission) a question like 'will I be paid?' immediately labels you as a beginner and, in a tough and competitive business where there are many experienced writers also looking for work, you don't want to broadcast the fact that you are inexperienced. (Note: You should always imply that you expect to be paid!)

This means knowing something about the types of contracts and deals that exist in television. In this chapter I shall describe the main types of television contracts for drama series and serials (which include soaps) you are likely to come across.

Although this is a book about television, I shall include feature film agreements because many single films for television (usually filling a 90-minute or 120-minute slot) started off life as would-be feature films (and vice versa). Famously, *Four Weddings and a Funeral* was intended as a television movie with modest expectations but in the event it became a massive cinema hit, grossing about £250m worldwide.

I shall also describe a relatively simple back-of-the-envelope way to negotiate any deal for a single script (i.e. not for a television series episode but for a movie or television movie). With this information it is possible to talk authoritatively to any producer suggesting you are professional and understand the business.

## Why you need to understand contracts

Writers are freelance business people; their contracts commit them to all sorts of terms and conditions. Failure to observe or understand the terms can result in serious consequences: contracts can be invalidated; writers can get fired; and – most commonly – the writer can end up getting paid less than they would from a better-negotiated contract.

Proper understanding of your contracts will gain you the respect of producers who are good to work with and will make the bad ones more careful with you. It's worth noting here that not all producers are equal and you want to be wary of producers who perhaps need you more than you need them. This is not always easy to gauge if you meet at a film festival, but Google or IMDb will usually reveal whether they have produced anything before.

They may be excellent people, with great integrity, but they may have little money and even less experience, and so may not be an asset to your career. That being said, there are times when it is better to have such a person trying to set up a project based on your script, than to have the script sitting on your hard drive or shelf. The key thing is to make sure you can get the rights to the script back on as favourable terms as possible in the event that they do not get the project off the ground in the agreed time. This scenario is dealt with in detail later.

## Types of contract

In a chapter like this it is not possible to give an exhaustive analysis of the whole range of writers' contracts. For a start, film contracts can differ in many respects from television drama contracts. For example, television contracts generally fall into the soap (serial) or series category where usually only the money is negotiable (all the other terms are standard), but in film contracts there is much that is up for grabs. Film contracts for very low-budget films are different to standard film contracts (because of the higher level of deferrals or only nominal sums being paid). There is a further subdivision that covers contracts for scripts that are commissioned as opposed to scripts that have been written on spec and are therefore optioned.

Chapters 8 and 9 therefore describe – from an industry standpoint – the kinds of contract that you will hopefully encounter and suggests ways of preparing to respond to the terms you have been offered.

## The Writers' Guild of Great Britain

Many writers with agents (but particularly those without) find that the Writers' Guild of Great Britain (WGGB) is an invaluable organisation. The Guild is the central body negotiating the minimum terms for TV agreements with the broadcasters and independent producers on behalf of writers, so it is well worth being a member if you can. They also provide full members with a pension scheme, a free contract vetting service and a valuable weekly email newsletter.

Television drama contracts for shows like *EastEnders* are negotiated between the Writers' Guild and the BBC and are relatively straight-forward. Only the basic rate of pay varies, and is negotiable depending on your previous credits. The BBC has scales for different levels of credit. BBC contracts differ from ITV, which differ from those used by independent producers. The rates and basic terms are all available on the WGGB website (www.writersguild.org.uk). The fact that you can access these without being a member should *not* make you think you do not need to join the Guild: being a member is an immediate indicator of professionalism and also gives you access to a team of extremely knowledgeable and dedicated people who are there to help you in your career. The Guild puts on some of the best events for sharing information and networking. They have regional officers in different parts of the country so that if you are in the Midlands or Scotland or Cornwall you will find like-minded people always ready with information, advice and camaraderie.

For less experienced writers there is student membership and candidate membership, which is for those without the necessary credit to allow them full membership. In the absence of an agent, joining the Guild is invaluable. Go to meetings, read their literature, spend time on their website, follow them on Twitter and read their blog. It is a very important statement to others about how you value your professionalism as a writer.

So a good place to start in order to get yourself more familiar with typical contracts is the WGGB website. Examples of all Guild contracts for television, film, theatre, radio and other formats are there in the 'About Us/Rates and Agreements' section. Below is the list of Guild television contracts with some guiding explanation from me.

- BBC Television Script Commissioning Agreement. (This is the template agreement that is used by the BBC when commissioning a script. Like all these agreements the terms have been negotiated by the Guild.)

- BBC TV minimum rates. (These are the minimum rates that the BBC has agreed to pay WGGB members. You should be able to insist on these rates even if you are not a WGGB member, although there are producers who cannot afford to pay even these minimums. You have to make a choice: to sell even at very low rates or not to sell? Later in this chapter we will look at ways of arranging contracts when there is little or no money on offer.)

- WGGB/PACT TV agreement. (Used with independent producers who are members of the Producers' Alliance for Cinema and Television.)

- WGGB/ITV/PMA agreement. (If the ITV broadcaster commissions a script this is the template agreement used.)

- Writers' Guild/TAC/S4C agreement. (Used for Channel 4 in Wales.)

- Writers' Guild/TAC/S4C rates. (Used for Channel 4 in Wales.)

There are also other Guild contracts on the WGGB website.

---

The WGGB website also hosts a document called 'Working With Writers – a good practice guide for TV programme makers' (2009). This is a very interesting document and well worth reading carefully about how writers should be treated by television companies.

---

## Seeking legal advice

If you think that there are serious legal or copyright issues that could affect you, take advice from an expert. The Writers' Guild – if you are a member – can get you free advice, which is a good reason for being a member. Read the legal pages in www.twelve point.com also known as *ScriptWriter* magazine (www.twelvepoint. com) for additional advice. Or talk to a lawyer. There are organisations like Blue Pencil Media who give legal advice to writers (www. bluepencilset.com).

Do not use a high-street law firm unless they have a media specialist. Media law is specialised. Lawyers charge by the hour (or part thereof) so can be costly and you have to pay when they do the work, as opposed to agents, who take their commission when you get paid.

## Copyright

Copyright is a minefield but fortunately for you it is one that writers need not know a great deal about. The two key things you should be aware of are as follows.

- Copyright automatically exists in anything you write as long as you have not copied it illegally from anyone else. (You should never use anyone else's material without their permission – which you should get in writing). So written material like an original script of yours is automatically your copyright. However, the title of your script, particularly if it is very short, or a phrase in wider use like The Heist or Love Story or Spooks, may not be copyrighted.
- Copyright continues until 70 years after the end of the year of the death of the writer.

Copyright will be referred to in all your contracts because at a certain point you will need to assign (a legal term for selling) the copyright in your work to the producer or broadcaster. If you want to know more about copyright there is an excellent chapter in the *Writers' & Artists' Yearbook*, which is published annually by A&C Black.

# 7 Options

## What to look out for in an option agreement, what happens when an option is exercised, and should you ever agree to a free option?

Options are the most common basis for writers' agreements and if you are familiar and even confident about dealing with a negotiation at this stage, you will give a professional and businesslike impression, making good producers more inclined to want to work with you.

## Why do we have options?

Producers have great trouble raising the money to make films or television programmes so they don't want to buy (actually pay the full purchase price for) the rights to a book or script until they have found out whether they can actually raise the money to make the film or show.

They therefore introduced an interim stage that costs them less: this is called the 'option'. It is the option to buy the rights to make the film or TV show. So producers buy an exclusive option to a book, treatment, play or script (so no one else can buy it) while they see if they can get the project off the ground, get a script commissioned if there isn't one, identify a director, find suitable casting and raise the finance to do any or all of these things.

It would not be worth undertaking all the effort involved in doing these things unless the producer knew they had exclusive access to buy the rights. Optioning is therefore not actually buying the rights to make the programme but buying the exclusive right to buy those rights to make a film or television programme based on the work optioned. A producer who does not protect themself like this is unlikely to be any good at protecting all the investors and therefore may be worth being wary of!

An option agreement only applies to a previously written copyright document (which could be a treatment, short story, article, novel or script). If a producer or broadcaster commissions a writer, perhaps even with an idea provided by the person commissioning, then there is nothing to option.

For example, if a producer says to a writer that they want a bank robbery drama for prime-time television, in which the robbery goes wrong because the robber is a cat lover and stops to help a lost kitten, the conversation or idea is not copyrightable. If they write it down, it is, because copyright exists in material form, such as writing or musical notes or a drawing or sculpture.

Bear in mind, however, that if they state that they are telling you the idea in confidence (and can prove it later, perhaps there is a third person witness) then you may not use that idea without their involvement even if there is no copyright involved. Doing so would be a 'breach of confidentiality', which is a good defence against having ideas stolen that are verbally communicated. Copying something written down could be breach of copyright.

## The option agreement

You should have the basics of an option deal clear in your mind, and note that there are four key parts to an option agreement.

An option is (1) the exclusive right to acquire (2) certain rights (usually related to the making of a film or television drama) for (3) an agreed sum of money and for (4) an agreed length of time. All of these elements must be stated for the option to be binding.

The agreed length of time of an option can vary, as can the number of options that a producer might want, depending on how the project is progressing. Typically, options are 12 or 18 months long, and there are usually two or three in a row. So a script being under option for 36 months would be fairly common.

The producer has to 'renew' the option (i.e. from the moment the first ends and the second begins) and to do this they should pay an additional fee that should have been agreed when the contract was originally negotiated. It is common for the second option to be the same price as the first and the third the same price as the second, (though this isn't a hard and fast rule).

The first option payment is deducted from the purchase price or is described as being 'set against' the purchase price. The third option payment (and sometimes the second) are usually in addition to the purchase price. (The purchase price is the total amount, not including profits or residuals, payable on or before the first day of principal photography.)

Should an option period run out without the appropriate payment to renew it or without the producer paying the purchase price, the producer should automatically lose the rights to the material and they revert to the writer. You should never repay option payments when the producer loses the rights.

Producers often find it difficult to raise the money for a production so they need as long a period of time as possible. Personally I think that two years option with one producer is long enough; three should be the maximum.

The rights granted to producers are typically partial copyright. Think of copyright as a bundle of separate (but related) rights; these can include the right to make a programme or film, the right to stage a play based on the material written or make a radio play, the right to publish a book, the right to make merchandising objects or computer games.

You may have to option *all* these rights to a producer who is in a strong position but you may be able to withhold or reserve some. Usually the contract will state that all audiovisual and allied rights, including stage plays, radio, publishing etc. are being assigned by the writer to the producer. You can try to reserve some of these rights although the producer may insist that you not be able to utilise them for a number of years. This is called a 'holdback'.

Note, however, that an option does not give the producer the right to make the drama or movie; it gives the producer the right to acquire the rights necessary to make the drama or movie. This is an important distinction. However, the option will include the right to raise money towards making the production, the right to commission treatments and scripts, and seek directors, casting and so on, but not the right to make the production.

The rights to actually make the drama or movie are covered by another document – the 'purchase' agreement – also known as the 'assignment' or sometimes 'exercise' agreement. This is usually appended to the option agreement. Typically all the terms of the purchase agreement are negotiated at the same time as the terms of the option agreement, so all the producer has to do to acquire the rights to *make* the production is to give the owner of the rights notice that that is what is about to happen *and* to pay the money agreed as the purchase or exercise price. (See the next section on 'Exercising an option' for more detail on this.)

### Performance-related clauses

You can sometimes include performance-related clauses in contracts forcing the producer to be active or risk losing the right to renew the option. Without certain goals that you want the producer to achieve, they could just sit on your material, which is aggravating if they have not paid you very much for it. This is therefore a way to try to impose on them the fact that if they are optioning (for example) a treatment by you, then in order to renew the option for a second option period they have to pay you more money or commission the script from you.

Say, for example, the producer has relatively little money and they want your spec script (a script you wrote without any commission to do so) but all they can offer is £100 for a 12- or 18-month option.

You insist that if they want the option to the script (of which they claim to think highly), then within the first 12 or 18 months they must demonstrate enough professionalism to have raised, say, £1,000 (or even more) in order to renew the option. Failure to pay you that money means the option lapses and automatically returns to you without your having to repay the money (if that is what the contract you sign with the producer stipulates).

Option money paid to a writer should never have to be repaid if the option lapses. Dig your heels in on this. Alas when an option is exercised (see below) then the money paid to you (which includes the option payments) is usually repayable if the film is not made (usually within five or seven years) and you want the rights back.

## Exercising an option

As explained above, the option contract goes together with another important document, the exercise or purchase or assignment contract, which is the one that actually transfers to the producer the rights to make the film. These words – purchase, exercise or assignment – are (confusingly) interchangeable. The purchase price can also be called the 'exercise' price or the 'assignment' price.

Let's assume that you are now at the moment when the producer chooses to exercise the option. This is usually because since the option of your script, the producer has hopefully been working very hard raising money, finding cast and lining up crew. A moment then arrives when the producer believes that they can greenlight the film or programme (or at least they convince themselves that they can).

Exercising an option is what happens when the producer actually purchases the rights necessary to make the production. They have to do this before the option or the extended option expires or before the first day of principal photography, whichever is the sooner.

It is normal for the writer to be paid a far bigger sum of money at the point of exercise than they were paid on option (or on the renewal/s of the option/s). As mentioned above, both the option agreement and the assignment are usually drawn up at the same time. In other words, both parties agree – at the time that the option is signed – about the details of the purchase. When the option part of the contract is signed, the 'assignment' (or exercise/purchase) part of the contract is only initialled (usually on every page). It is signed on exercise when the writer should receive the agreed exercise payment.

This means that the writer cannot unilaterally withdraw from the whole deal once the option is signed or stop the producer from exercising the option if, for example, the writer no longer likes them or doesn't trust them. All the producer has to do to exercise the option or purchase the rights is to give notice and pay the money due.

This is a crucial aspect of contracts to bear in mind. If you are asked to sign an option agreement which says that in the event that the film is likely to go ahead, other terms will be negotiated in good faith, be careful. In such circumstances, when the producer comes with the good news, you can insist on being paid £1m for the rights or they can say that the film can only be made if you accept £1,000. Either way you are both in a difficult and unprofessional situation. So insist on at least having the option agreement state that you will not receive less than, for example, 2% of the certified budget (i.e. the official budget of the production) as your fee if the film is made. The 2% might be 1.5% or 2.5% depending on your negotiating power.

## Payment for copyright to your work

You should refuse to allow the copyright to pass to the producer while all they have is an option. They don't really need it however much they might argue that they do. They should only get it when two things happen: (1) when they notify you that they are exercising the option, and (2) when they simultaneously pay you the exercise price. Without your receiving the money, copyright should not pass.

Most producer-originated contracts state that non-payment does not constitute a fundamental breach of the agreement and that you cannot withdraw from the agreement because of it. Instead you must sue them in a court for the money. Sadly, there is not much you can do about this but by holding on to the copyright until you are paid, you ensure that they will pay you the exercise price or at least the delivery of the first draft script money (i.e. the money payable when you deliver the first draft of the script), without you having to chase them for it. Use this as a negotiating lever to ensure you get paid for the delivery sooner rather than later.

The producer will have to own the copyright to the work at some point. To access some public funds it might have to be earlier rather than later because some government subsidy funding for script development requires producers to own the underlying rights (including the copyright) and this is sometimes put up as collateral against the loan of the money.

So if you can, to protect yourself, ask for a clause to be added that the producer pays interest at perhaps 2% above base rate if they are more than 14 days late with a payment, and that your delivery of the next draft is extended by the length of time that they are late in paying for the previous draft.

You should never assign copyright to a producer in perpetuity. They should own the rights for, say, five or seven years and if the first day of principal photography has not commenced before the five or seven years from the date that the exercise of the option starts, then the rights come back to you.

Whether it is five or seven years (or whatever is negotiated) depends on how much the producer has paid and how strong your negotiating position is. If three companies want to buy your script you are in a better position to shorten the time period than if it has been knocking around for years with no one wanting to buy it until now when just one producer is interested.

If the time agreed lapses without the production being made you will usually have to pay back what they have paid to purchase the rights from you. Try to resist paying more than they have paid you. Sometimes the money they raised to pay you was on terms including interest, so they will force you to accept that you will have to pay them back the interest on top of what they paid you. This means making sure that the amount you have to pay back is limited in your contract when you first negotiate.

Note that the copyright in *their* film or TV show (if they produced it) based on your script remains theirs even if copyright in your script reverts to you after an agreed number of years.

## An option example

So now you know some of the basics about options and exercise, let's look at an example and see how fluid negotiations can be. Say you have written a treatment and a producer wants to option it. There are several things that you can do to improve the contract at this point. (Note: A good producer may well offer reasonable or even good terms without having to be asked but it is not common!)

The first option payment is almost always 'set against' the purchase or exercise price. This means that if the option for the first year is £500 and the purchase price is £10,000, then in order to exercise the option before the 12 months expires the producer has to pay you £9,500. (These figures are a little arbitrary – check the WGGB website for the current minimum figures that you should try to adhere to if you can't argue for a higher set of figures.)

The second-year option, however, is sometimes *not* set against the purchase price. So, if the producer wants to keep your property off the market for a second year, then the second option payment, which may be another £500, is not set against the purchase price. This means that having paid you £1,000 for the two one-year options, the producer still has to pay you £9,500 to exercise the option, making a total of £10,500 not the £10,000 you would have received had the option been exercised during the first year. So you have made an extra £500!

If there is a third-year option, it should definitely not be set against the purchase price. In fact, I believe that the option payment for a third period should be significantly higher than for the first two. By now, if the producer has not raised any money at all on your script or treatment, then there are serious doubts about their ability to do so.

You should never have to repay option money you have received if an option expires. If the producer does not exercise the option, the producer loses all rights to acquire the script or book and you should automatically get them back.

Remember: avoid options running on for too long. Two or maybe three years is reasonable. You should, though, impose conditions on extensions, such as agreeing to the second or the third year on condition that there has been some progress, as mentioned above.

If you are a scriptwriter and have sold a treatment in a one-year option agreement, then I certainly think that it is reasonable for you to be commissioned to write the script before the year or first option period is out. Otherwise why sell them the option?

Sometimes producers will buy a treatment or script but insist from the start that another writer – usually a well-known A-list writer – will take over the script. It might be worth doing this because a higher-profile and successful programme will benefit your career profile, and you will get payment and credit.

## Fighting your corner

Here are some good ways of putting pressure on the producer, especially if they have not paid you well up front.

If the producer is a one-person company and can only pay peanuts and they need the option in order to interest a bigger player, such as a broadcaster, try to limit them in the first instance to an option of three or six months. Upon evidence that there is some progress in raising the money, the period could be automatically extended, by perhaps another 12 months. You can insist that you receive details of all submissions of your script made by the producer, and responses to those submissions (i.e. usually the reasons for them being rejected).

A producer who acquires a treatment or script for nothing and then uses it to set up a production is doing nothing wrong, although they are, in effect, using your material to get themselves work. In this scenario you are in a kind of partnership and information should be properly shared. You are also an 'investor' in the production and the fact that you have agreed to defer what you should have been paid should be reflected in the contract by your getting more than the script fees, such as a bigger profit share. So if you get no payments until the first day of principal photography, instead of a standard 2% of the producer's net profits you may be able to get 4%. But don't spend it before you receive it as most films never make a profit!

## Free options

We will now look at a difficult subject: free options. These come up frequently, especially with relatively inexperienced and uncredited writers and also when treatments are being written.

A quick aside – much of what follows in this section relates to a single TV drama or film in an agreement with an independent producer. A deal with a broadcaster will usually be along the lines of the template contracts on the WGGB website. However, as very few writers work only on television and, as many films are written on spec or commissioned for television, the basic deal structure that is outlined below will apply to scripts which may end up on TV even if they were not conceived for TV (or may end up on cinema screens even though intended for television). There is no clear distinction and the negotiating strategies overlap both industries.

You meet a producer or they seek you out. You discuss ideas and agree that one of your or their ideas is worth developing. The producer offers to put a great deal of energy and time (and there-fore money) into finding finance to get this project off the ground but there is not much money (if any) for you. Because you would love to have a chance to write the script and have a film made based on it, you are tempted to do this for the producer without any payment. It seems like a great opportunity. Is it worth getting involved on this basis?

Well, film and TV production is a tough business, with not enough profit being made by most people working in it. One consequence of this is that there isn't enough development money, meaning writers have to invest their time and ideas for free in order to provide producers with something with which to raise money.

Both writers and producers are in a difficult position. A normal Writers' Guild script agreement assumes that the producer has the money to pay for the writer to do the work. The fact is that quite often this is not the case.

So, writers work on spec (for nothing, or next to nothing) or to commission without pay, until delivery of the script or even the first day of principal photography, something to be avoided if at all possible. In my mind that makes them partners or investors, who should have the right to receive more than just the scriptwriters' payments. In this scenario, the writer is investing in the film or in the producer just as if he or she had given the producer money. So producers will sometimes offer additional benefits such as a higher profit share or additional credits (such as associate producer or even co-producer) and if they don't, you need to ask for them during the negotiation. Don't leave it until after the contract is signed to raise these questions.

You could also (or alternatively) ask for an extra few thousand pounds or perhaps an extra 5% (or 10% of your total fee) or if it is a higher-budget film, then ask for an additional £5,000 or even £10,000 on the first day of principal photography in addition to your normal deal. By then it is not the producer's money. If the producer refuses because the broadcaster won't agree, ask for a bigger share of the producer's profits. You definitely should receive something extra.

But if they say that they can't pay anything extra, or give you an additional credit (sometimes it is easier to get this than more money), then if you believe that the producer is capable of realising the production, go ahead and sign. We do not always win every point in a negotiation.

It is not an ideal situation but if you trust the producer and you want your project to be developed by the producer – rather than gather dust on your shelves – then it is a calculated risk probably worth taking.

---

**Option negotiation checklist**

This is a brief summary of the most important points to remember and consider when you are looking at an option negotiation.

1. How much is paid for the option? If you are offered £1, ask for £1,000 with £999 deferred until the producer enters into an agreement with a third party (film fund, co-production partner or whoever).
2. How long is the option?
3. Can the option be renewed, for how long and how often?
4. Are any of the option payments not included in the purchase price?
5. Remember that option payments are never repaid if the producer does not proceed with the film.
6. You must be able to mention immediately the sale of the option (or the commission) in your CV and discuss any

---

aspect of it with your professional advisers. Contracts usually have onerous confidentiality clauses but make sure that you have the right to do these two things written into your contract.

7. Do you have the right of first refusal to write the script based on your treatment (or second draft if your first draft was optioned)? In other words, make sure that no other writer can be brought in until you have had a chance to do the next stage to prove you are capable of it. If you don't deliver an acceptable draft then you might be fired.

8. Do you automatically get the rights back without repayment if the option expires? Or if the option is exercised, can you still get them back after an agreed number of years? What repayment is then necessary?

## The purchase price

A key element in the purchase/exercise/assignment agreement that many writers and producers, early on in the negotiations, do not know how to assess, is what the purchase or exercise price should be. There is, fortunately, a commonly accepted rule of thumb for it. It is not simple or straightforward, but read through to the end of this section and hopefully it will be clear enough. A specific example is given to demonstrate the rule of thumb. It is well worth getting a working understanding of this because for most scriptwriters this is one of the most common negotiations that they will have in their career.

Earlier in this chapter I said that the first and second (usually not the third) option payment is deductible from the purchase price.

The amount paid for options varies but about 5% of the purchase price is fairly common and accepted these days. Try to insist on no less than 5%.

The purchase price amount is usually 'an agreed minimum guaranteed purchase price (also known as the floor/minimum guarantee), or a percentage of the total production's budget, whichever is the greater'. There is usually a maximum (ceiling) of about three or four times the floor or minimum guarantee because if the script attracts a better cast, the writer should not have their proportion of the budget reduced, hence the essential fairness of using a percentage of the budget. While it can happen that the overall budget increases by more than three or four times, which would reduce the writer's proportion, this is rare, and a ceiling of three or four times the floor is normally considered acceptable.

The basic purchase price percentage is usually between 2% and 3% of the total above- and below-the-line budget for the whole production. A producer should not pay more than 5% for both the underlying rights (if there is also, for example, a novel or a book which they have to buy rights for) and the script. The industry accepts a maximum of 5% as reasonable and normal.

A 'beginner' scriptwriter, i.e. one with few or no credits, might receive as little as 1% or 1.5% of the budget, whereas a more experienced writer would receive 2% to 3%.

Knowing this, it is relatively easy to arrive at the minimum and maximum purchase price. You need to start with the production budget. In many cases the producer will say that, at this early stage in the process, they do not know what the budget is, so we need to guess. They are probably telling the truth here but they must have a rough idea of what they are likely to raise and how much this type of film is likely to cost. If they don't have a rough idea at all, be a little wary of them; they might be inexperienced or too manipulative!

Don't concede at every negotiating point because you fear losing the deal. Gently explore how far you push them. You might be pleasantly surprised. And if you lose a deal from time to time you will probably make more money overall. Producers who pull out at the slightest resistance to their offers are usually not easy to work with.

The beauty of the formula I am going to describe is that it takes into account all these difficulties the producer has in being too definite about the budget.

> A professional writer should also roughly know how budgets are made up and what a script is likely to cost to film. See www.twelvepoint.com archive for an article on what writers should know about budgets.

So, let's say that it is likely to be a £1.5m production budget. If the writer has many credits then, as I mentioned, they should receive at least 2.5% of the budget; if they are a beginner, maybe 1% or 1.5%. Let's assume our writer has a couple of credits and will receive 2%.

Two percent of £1.5m is £30,000. So the minimum purchase price (as long as the writer is the sole writer of the script that is shot) is £30,000. The maximum, in the event that the budget goes up, could be three or even four times that. Let's say it is three times giving a maximum purchase price of £90,000.

If, however, the writer is fired after a couple of drafts and another writer is brought in, then the final payment will work out less than stated above because some (the amount or proportion agreed at the time the contract is first negotiated) of the total will be paid to the new writer.

For now, the basic deal (or the formula) can be summed up in this way: producer buys the rights from writer to script X for a guaranteed minimum of £30,000 or 2% of the certified budget whichever is the greater, with a ceiling, or maximum, of £90,000.

If the option is 5% of the minimum purchase price for 18 months that will be £1,500. The option will be renewable for a further 18 months for the same sum. Try to ensure that the second option payment is not deducted from the purchase price. Sometimes you will succeed, sometimes you will not.

This formula protects the writer in the event that the TV programme or film is made for a higher budget (a great script attracting a higher and more expensive calibre of actors and director), but the producer is also protected in case the budget soars: without the ceiling, producers insist that they would have trouble financing the film. (They say this rather too often for me to believe them all the time – like the little boy who cried wolf – but it is a buyers' market so writers and their agents generally have little leverage.)

There are always nuances and refinements or variations, which is why in one chapter it is so difficult to cover all there is to say on writers' contracts. For example, the budget is usually defined to exclude certain items such as the contingency budget, the completion bond (see Glossary on page 263 for definitions of these), fees paid to the writer of the script, financing charges and insurance. Producers try to include other items in the exclusions such as an overhead element and legal fees, which writers and writers' agents should resist. The 'usual exclusions' should approximately amount to 12% to 15% of the budget.

## What about profits?

Whole books could be written and many pages in contracts are used to cover definitions of profits. Writers do not usually receive a share of the film's profits; they tend to receive a share of the producer's profits (commonly less than 20% of the film's profits *if* the film makes any profits at all – most don't!). The percentage of the producer's profits given to the writer depends on several factors such as how much the writer deferred up front (if the producer could only pay a modest or nominal option, then the writer is in fact deferring until later fees that they should have received earlier) and on how important the writer is (the number of credits the writer has). The figure is usually between 2% and 5% of the producer's net profits.

You should try to obtain a profit clause but don't expect to earn anything from it. Very few films or television programmes make profits. It will then be a nice surprise if some revenues do come in!

It should also be mentioned that producers who have managed to raise some of the finance for the production of the film, but run out of agreed option periods, will try to re-negotiate an additional option period extension beyond those agreed in the contract.

You can refuse this request even if they offer to pay (that is if you want to take the rights back from them and prevent them from continuing to try to make the film). They do have the right (until the expiry) to pay the whole purchase price if they choose to and can afford to. This is not common but it does happen.

If you decide to agree to an extension to the option try to get them to pay double what they paid for the previous option: after all they are keeping your property off the market for a longer time.

# 8 Commissions

## How to ensure you get a good deal when you are asked to write a script from scratch

Having dealt with negotiating to buy the rights to a script, let's now look at how different it is when a producer *commissions* a script that does not exist. They could also be commissioning a treatment or even a pitch or selling document describing the proposed script, but because of the ubiquity of single script deals, I will be looking at them in detail as many of them end up on television. Let's start with a single script commission, then we will look at TV episode commissions.

The commissioning of a script may occur where an option of a treatment already exists. If there is an existing copyright work then strictly it should be optioned or purchased, otherwise a commissioned script based on a treatment that the producer does not own could lead to problems – for example, the underlying work (the treatment) could be sold to someone else.

It is usual, if there is no pre-existing treatment, for a producer to commission one. Then there might be a step outline (a more detailed scene-by-scene treatment) before the first draft script is commissioned. Usually you can insist on writing the step outline or first draft script if it is your treatment on which they are based. However, if you are a complete beginner or a prose writer then a more experienced TV writer might be brought in to do this.

If the producer came up with the script idea (and therefore owns it) and a writer creates the script on spec then if the producer does not make the film, the writer cannot usually sell the script they have written because the writer doesn't own the underlying rights. So writing for nothing or for very little is more risky if it is not based on an idea of your own. If the idea and script were originated by the writer and the producer fails to make the film within an agreed time, all rights should revert to the writer who is then free to sell the script, as described above.

If a producer has an idea but wants you to write the script for next to nothing, you should ensure that the deal memo (a brief form of contract which usually states that a longer and more complete contract will be agreed at a later stage, before principal photography) or contract contains a clause to the effect that if they do not exercise the rights within the agreed timeframe, then all rights in the script and in their original idea revert to you, and if you get the film set up you will pay them something for the idea (say 10% of what you receive for the script). Unless there is a document providing that it is legally yours to sell on to another producer, you will not be able to prove 'chain of title' and will thus not be able to sell it.

The WGGB/PACT agreement (1992) is primarily for film not television but it is useful as a benchmark for any commission for an original single script. It has a clear breakdown for the stages of payment.

1. Commission of treatment: 10% of the total fee payable on the first day of principal photography.

2. Acceptance of treatment: 10%. (Acceptance means they can ask for several rewrites; always insist on written notes prior to a rewrite to establish exactly what it is they want changed).

3. Commission of first draft script: 20%.

4. Delivery of first draft script: 20%.

5. Commission of second draft script: 10%.

6. Acceptance of second draft script: 10% (i.e. they can ask for many rewrites).

7. First day of principal photography: 20%. (If you are fired after the first draft – see below for more on this – the second draft money is usually paid to another writer and if, say, each writer is responsible for 50% of the shooting script, then the principal photography payment is split 50/50.)

This agreement is used for single films for television as well as for feature films, since it is not always clear at the outset whether the film is going to end up on the big or small screen. There is often the intention that it will be a feature film for cinemas, but in fact it ends up on television and DVD only. So this is a very useful template for all scriptwriters to be familiar with.

The Writers' Guild has published an advisory booklet called 'Writing Film – a good practice guide for screenwriters and those who work with them' (2009) because the PACT/Writers' Guild Agreement could not be renegotiated. This complements the Guild's good practice guide for TV programme makers.

Television series or soap episode commissions differ in several respects: firstly, if it is an episode of *EastEnders* or *Coronation Street* you will usually be given the basic storyline that will have been agreed by an inner circle of writers and the production team. So while there may be some room to show what you are worth, being faithful to character and storyline are paramount.

You may be asked to do an extended treatment based on the storyline, and when that is approved you will be asked to do the first of what is likely to be several drafts of the script.

The problem is that you may get script notes from different people at different times requiring more work to be done by you (for no more money) than was really necessary. But if you think of the complexity of the production line, with unmoveable transmission dates and several episodes which have to dovetail being written by different writers, you might wonder why anyone wants the job of co-ordinating that.

So take the deadlines seriously; make sure you understand exactly what is wanted of you in each rewrite – if you are not sure email your understanding and ask for confirmation. The reality is that most first drafts don't work – a fact of scriptwriting life. It happens with TV scripts and also with film scripts. In my opinion the original writer should always be given the right to do the second draft once they have received detailed notes from the producer. In other words, before the writer can be fired they should be given one set of notes and the chance to make the second draft a better one, thus keeping them on the project as the only writer and therefore not having to share any of the script fees or credits.

Sadly it is quite common for writers to be fired off projects, including ones that they had originated. And it is fairly common on TV episodes if time is running out. Never fail to warn the producer if you think you will not hit delivery date on a soap, even by a couple of days. Far better to warn them as soon as you realise there is a problem: that way they are more likely to trust you and try to keep you in the picture as the writer. If you make their job more difficult by not saying something you could have said, they will feel far less inclined to work with you again.

Most agreements pay the writer on commencement of the writing and on delivery or acceptance of the draft. Writers prefer payment 'on delivery'; producers prefer to pay on acceptance. It is more usual for the early drafts to be paid on delivery but the final draft on acceptance, which enables the producer to ask for additional polishes on the final draft without having to pay the next stage until it is accepted.

Soap and series agreements usually pay half on commencement, and the rest on delivery with the buyout amount being paid on transmission. There are variations to this. Negotiating your fee is very dependent on your credits: the producers and broadcasters have rates that relate specifically to how many credits you have and there is very little negotiating leeway.

Some agreements stipulate the 'reading time' that the producer has before they need to go back and accept or ask for more work on the draft. Writers cannot be expected to keep themselves available for months until the producer gives notes or asks for a new draft; on the other hand, producers want the writer to be available to them, usually at short notice and exclusively. On average, a reading time of two to four weeks is common.

I recommend asking for script feedback in the form of written notes as a matter of course so that if there is a dispute about whether a rewrite is acceptable, it is possible to see objectively whether the writer has done what they were asked to do. Also, if the producer 'moves the goalposts', i.e. asks for changes that were never part of the agreed treatment or storyline or previous notes, the writer (or agent) can try to insist on a 'rebrief fee'. This is sometimes in addition to the contracted amount due and takes the sting out of doing a great deal of extra work unpaid (though sometimes it might simply bring forward some of the contracted payments and not be additional to the previously agreed total).

---

Try to avoid having to be available on 'exclusive first call' if possible, unless you are being paid very well. Exclusive first call means that if they need you to work on their project it has to take precedence over any other work you may have. So just state that you would love to be exclusively theirs but as you can't live on what they are paying you, that is not possible. Reasonable availability is fine, perhaps also subject to your other professional commitments. It is sensible to ask for four weeks to write a draft (or however long you think it might take) when in fact you can deliver in three weeks.

---

## Reserving certain rights

Rights that are commonly reserved to the writer (i.e. not sold to the producer as part of their purchase of copyrights) are usually publishing, radio and stage exploitation of the work. Traditionally, however, the producer insists on a 'holdback' preventing the writer from exploiting them for three or five years after exercise. This is old-fashioned and benefits neither side; you should argue for greater flexibility, but producers are usually conservative and you won't often succeed.

Unless you have an agent or are sufficiently proactive in being able to sell these rights yourself, you might let the producer control them. As a matter of negotiating principle, however, I would advise you not to: if the TV show or film is a success another company may want to buy one or more of the rights you reserved and you, rather than the first producer, can make money from this and perhaps ensure that you get to write the adaptation.

## Remake and sequel rights

Traditionally a remake earns the original writer one third of the original purchase fee, and a sequel earns the writer 50%. Tradition is hard to argue against and it is a Hollywood tradition where the first fee was often a great deal of money. When the fee is modest, the one third or one half is unfair to the writer as remakes and sequels usually happen a number of years after the original by which time inflation will have reduced the value of the fee significantly. Also, because few producers will make a remake or sequel unless the first version was successful, there is less risk for the producer. Instead, I would suggest 1.66% or 2% of the budget (as opposed to one third or one half of the original purchase fee) which is a reasonable compromise, with a floor measured in the same way as the original agreement if possible.

## Getting back your rights

One important clause that causes anxiety in purchase agreements and is worth fighting over is that relating to reversion or 'turnaround'.

Reversion is when you get back your rights, i.e. they revert to you. For example, you may have insisted that if principal photography does not occur for, say, five years after the exercise of the option, then the producer loses the right to make the film and all rights in your script revert to you.

In some contracts (often in the USA) there is a turnaround window in which you have, say, a year in which you can repurchase the rights i.e. return any fee you have received. If you don't do it or have someone else to do it in that year, you might lose the right to reclaim your rights. This is to be avoided at all costs if possible. Make it a deal breaker. Bluff to the brink; it sometimes works. (If it doesn't you can still sell them your work, but at least you have tried to improve the deal.)

In most contracts, in order to enable you to sell your script to someone else, you have to pay back the first producer the money they paid you on exercising the option. The repayment to the first producer is usually on the first day of principal photography of the film made by the new producer. There is much room for negotiating here and for big arguments. Personally I don't think there should be anything repaid to the producer. After all, they have had the rights to the script or book for five or seven years and they have failed to make the film. Why should they be rewarded? Why should the writer be penalised?

The main reasons that some repayment is probably inevitable are that it is a buyers' market so producers can insist on certain terms (like repayment). Also, subsidy-funded productions, and many film investment companies, require repayment, so this stipulation is passed on to the writer. If you don't accept it you could lessen the chances of selling your script.

An acceptable and fair compromise, in my opinion, is as follows.

1. After the five- or seven-year period has expired, the rights revert to the writer who can resell them.

2. On the first day of principal photography of the film (i.e. only if the script goes into production with another producer) the new producer must pay back to the first producer only the sums paid to the writer by the first producer and nothing more.

Another deal is that the writer agrees to pay back everything the producer wants at a rate of say 20% or even 50% of the money the writer receives from the new producer. This way the first producer will retrieve some of the money they expended but a deal where the whole amount must be repaid in a lump sum can often mean the writer will never sell the rights to their book or script again, and I think that is unacceptable. The reason for this is that if the first producer paid £50,000 for the rights to the script but the only producer who will buy the script seven years later is making a very low-budget version, £50,000 may be prohibitive and the writer may never sell it again, so the first producer will never recoup anything.

## Clauses to consider closely

The following are some other clauses you should be aware of and you should check carefully.

1. **Credits.** Writers should always be credited and there are usually industry-recognised credit provisions, such as 'Written by', or if you are the second writer of a pair who have worked on a script it might be 'Written with'. You always want 'front-end credits' (that is, before the film begins) rather than back-end credits. It is a good practice to insist on credits of a similar size and position

to the director and producer. Try to ensure that any script editor does not get copyright for any ideas that they contribute. Make sure that even if there is considerable input, only you actually write the script. So if you are presented with some dialogue written by the script editor or director, try not to cut and paste it, since it will by law be the writer's copyright not yours. Put it into your own words.

2. **Warranties.** Each party should make them, not only the writer. A warranty is a categorical statement that something is true and if you make a warranty about something in a contract and you are wrong about it (even inadvertently) it is a serious breach of the contract and the repercussions could be significant. The kinds of things you will warrant are that your work (in the script) is original to you, that it does not defame anyone, or breach anyone's privacy, that you have not sold it to anyone else and so on. You also have to agree to indemnify the other side if you are in breach of your warranties. Each party should provide indemnities in the event that the party is in breach of a warranty. Always try to resist having to indemnify against 'alleged breaches' of your warranties. An alleged breach is not (yet) a breach. Dig your heels in about this point. If the producer (or another writer) makes changes to the script and someone sues on that, you should be indemnified by them if you are sued for their contribution to the script.

3. **Disputes.** There should be a clause dealing with how disputes are to be resolved.

4. **Expenses/*per diems*.** This is a small point but it can be the cause of major problems! Expenses should be paid when the writer is not working from home. All travel and board and lodging costs

should be paid by the producer if the writer is expected to be more than 30 miles from their place of work (usually home). But bar bills are not usually paid!

5. **Confidentiality.** You may also be asked to keep every aspect of the deal confidential. There are two points to make here: the first is that you are legally entitled to discuss *any* part of the deal with your professional advisers (agent, lawyer, writing partner etc.); the second is you must be allowed to state the fact of the deal (if not any details) in your CV. Adding credits to your CV is a critically important way of making you more saleable as a writer.

This is not an exhaustive list of all the clauses in writers' contracts but they highlight many of the main points that frequently come up in the negotiations that take place between writer and producer or agent and producer.

# 9 Working with an agent

## How to choose, work with, change or do without an agent

Agents are sometimes perceived in a negative way. The people to whom agents sell work think that we charge too much and some clients think that we don't find them enough work (and probably that we also charge them too much!). Being in the middle has its inevitable downside. Furthermore, the days are long because reading is done outside office hours, so working over 80 hours a week is quite common.

However, most of the agents I know really enjoy their work. There are many uplifting moments and there is no other job I would rather do. We learn not to be personally affected by the rejections, even if they are for work that we care passionately about. We enjoy the successes, large and small and most clients at most agencies seem satisfied much of the time.

### Why have an agent?

Here are a few reasons why I think having an agent is valuable.

1. If you write well and handle your side of the relationship with your agent well, a good agent, like a good lawyer, or accountant, will earn you more money than they will cost you. So instead of

worrying about all the commission you are paying, think about the extra earnings you will have at the end of each year.

2. Most writers know there is a great deal of competition to get produced or published. A good agent should be able to cut through the competition to place the script or book into the hands of a buyer, and not just any buyer: the right buyer, who will then pay adequately before producing or publishing it well.

3. Good agents are regularly sought out by producers who want to know which writers they represent and what new material is available. A writer who joins a good agency can gain access to an immediate network of industry contacts.

Bear in mind: the agent *supplements* the proactive writer in the market, they do not replace them. Many agents won't take on a scriptwriter who is not out there networking, meeting producers, attending festivals like the London Screenwriters' Festival.

4. Some writers have full-time jobs and do not have the time to act for themselves. Many writers do not like the cut-and-thrust of negotiating or the legalese of contracts. For them it can be a relief to have an agent.

5. Some writers approach agents because many production companies refuse to consider work submitted directly. The production companies do this partly to avoid the danger of plagiarism suits. It also avoids having to read totally unsuitable material. If you receive a letter from a production company which says that they will only look at your material if it is submitted by an agent, it is their way of saying that they want another industry professional to vet it first. There is a presumption by production companies that if something is submitted by an agent it has at least been

read, that the agent thinks it might be good enough, and that it could be suitable for the producer in question.

> Just because your agent loves your work, that does not make it saleable. We do not always sell everything we like (or necessarily like everything we sell, although usually we like the writer), so don't assume that the hard work is over once an agent submits your work; you still need to be prepared to take some rejection and criticism.

Don't make the elementary mistake of thinking, as many writers do, that once they have an agent they can proceed with the writing and all the business, legal, tax and other aspects of their career will be fine. If it were true, writers would never leave their agents and agents would never fire their clients. Both do it reasonably often!

A writer is unable to acquire the breadth of experience on contracts and deals or the range and size of network if they only sell their own material. I may be biased but I think that agents can make a significant difference to their clients' careers, and most British and American writers who are reasonably successful choose to have agents.

## An agent and their contacts

One area where an agent ought to be of immediate benefit to a client is with their extensive network of contacts, both with potential buyers and with the industry in general.

You should look for an agent who is a member of various book, film and television associations and who is therefore well placed to gain further information about the industry that can be used to the benefit of their clients. For example, our agency is a member of:

- Association of Authors' Agents
- Romantic Novelists Association
- Society of Authors
- Society of Bookmen
- Crime Writers' Association
- Writers' Guild of Great Britain.

Writers should, for the same reasons, be active members of the relevant organisations and associations that exist for writers.

Apart from being able to find a buyer and hopefully being able to improve on an offer for a script, an agent should be able to help the client retain and exploit certain rights in the material.

If it is a script sale to a broadcaster, the agent might be better placed to limit their rights or licence and keep merchandising, publication or novelisation rights. Any good agent should be in a position to exploit these 'retained rights' on behalf of the client.

For many reasons, therefore, I believe that it is desirable and advantageous for a serious and professional writer to use an agent. As a team the sum is greater than the parts.

## When to get an agent

The complaint that is often heard in writers' groups is that you can't get an agent when you most need one, when you are starting, when you don't know what to write, who your audience is or what you should be paid. The harsh reality is that it is premature to expect an agent to take you on at this stage in your career.

Before getting an agent you need to win competitions, to get a relevant degree, do internships or work in the industry you want to write for. And you need to write a number of polished, saleable, calling card spec scripts, which might impress an agent.

The best time to start approaching agents, from the agent's point of view, is after you have begun to earn some money as a writer, have one or two commissions and have some relationships with producers. There is no hard and fast reason why you can't approach agents and producers at the same time, since it is impossible to predict which will produce the first result. Much depends on timing.

From a writer's point of view, if a production company announces (usually in the trades) that they are expanding and have hired a new producer or script editor, that is a good time to submit to them. However, agents don't usually make announcements about increasing their staff, so it is difficult to predict when is a good time to submit. And some production companies will not accept unagented scripts.

> Writers attract agents by what they have written, not, usually, by who they are. Sometimes a well-known person will be taken on by an agent because their name alone means that producers or publishers will see potential but it is the quality of the writing that is most important.

## Deciding which agent to choose

In the UK, the *Writers' & Artists' Yearbook* or *Cassell's Directory of Publishing* list most of the agents and they tell you which agents are members of the Association of Authors' Agents or the Personal Managers' Association. Agents have to have been in business for a certain number of years or have a turnover above a certain level to be admitted to the professional bodies representing agents. So it is a way of checking on the agent's standing. If you have a complaint about the agent you will also have an organisation (other than the WGGB) to which you can take your complaint.

In the *Writers' & Artists' Yearbook*, there is a brief paragraph on the agents' areas of interest and you can establish the commission rates and whether an agent charges a reading fee.

What such an entry does not tell you is if that agency is looking for clients or whether their list is full. Even if it is full, they may still take on a well-established writer or an inexperienced writer whom they think is brilliant, though most established agencies take on relatively few new clients in any one year.

You can also ask producers you work with if they can recommend anyone, but if you cannot get a recommendation, try identifying the writers whose work you most like and contact their agents. This, if nothing else, is an indication of your investigative abilities and can also be a little flattering to the agent. Your work, though, should be of a similar quality to the writers you admire.

If you know any writers, ask what they think of their agents and whether their agents are taking on new clients. If you don't know any other writers then join a writers' group. If you also want to write prose – something I would advise – try to find an agency that handles both prose and scripts.

It does help if you can write to the agent and say 'X or Y recommended me to write to you about representation' but make sure that X or Y is really known to the agent because at least once a month I'm told that someone whose name rings no bells has recommended the writer to me!

## How to approach agents

You can engineer 'chance' meetings with agents by networking. If you go to seminars and workshops, lectures and trade fairs, you will meet agents (the London Screenwriters' Festival is a particularly good event at which to meet agents). Usually they are reasonably happy to have a brief conversation about whether they are considering new clients but don't leap into a long pitch. Nothing puts an agent off as quickly as a writer who muscles in on a conversation the agent is having to offer them a script or manuscript. Although it may be a masterpiece, you are unlikely to endear yourself to the agent.

Remember also that if an agent is at a trade fair, they are working for existing clients and the time you take up detracts from that. Have a one-page description of your project and career to hand over. Make sure your name and contact details are on the sheet of paper (you would be surprised how often they are not).

### Cold calls

Personally I think you should not start by trying to talk to the agent on the phone. 'Cold calls' are not the best opener although some agents will take them. I will not talk to a prospective client unless I can read something first. From a phone call I suppose I might be able to tell the caller that the subject they have chosen doesn't suit or interest me or wouldn't, in my opinion, work in the marketplace. However, a letter or email takes a minute to read whereas a polite phone conversation can take 15 minutes. By talking to me they will not be taken more seriously so I prefer them to send something in to be read.

It is writing not telephone technique that counts at this point in the relationship. We receive over 100 applications from writers a week and obviously we cannot take cold calls from all these people. Apart from anything else, I need to be free to take calls from producers who are looking for writers!

### *Your covering letter*

It is essential to be able to tell the agent or producer succinctly the type of story you are writing or have written. If it is not right for the agent, you save yourselves time and money by establishing this at the outset. If you can summarise well, you've already provided the selling 'handle' and this may attract the agent.

There is a school of thought that recommends against sending in a script or treatment first. If your introductory letter is short and enticing, with a couple of good lines about the project, you should receive a request from the agency asking to see the material. This may create a sense of obligation in the agent to consider the material more carefully than if he or she had not requested it. However, I would argue, life is too short! I don't think it is more courteous to ask if the agent wants to see the material. Just don't bury them in it. Agents usually try to read submissions as quickly as they can. Their first reading priority should be to their existing clients, especially with material that has been commissioned or purchased. Only then should they read material from prospective clients. Do not send an entire novel, even if you have written it. If it is a script for a feature film or a 30- or 60-minute episode, then send the whole script and always include a short synopsis or treatment.

> There have been occasions when we have loved the quality of the writing in a script or chapter but not the idea or story. If all we had read was the treatment or synopsis, we would have rejected the material. We usually read some of both, though if we don't like the writing we will not read to the end.

In the covering letter you can also explain why you have written what you are submitting, whether you have been produced or published before and what your career aspirations are but don't oversell yourself. If you do you will be judged more harshly when the agent comes to read your submission.

You should also tell the agent how long the script or manuscript is (for a script, the length is usually only given in pages; for a manuscript, pages and word count should both be given). Some people think you should state whether the material submitted to the agent has been submitted to other agents, producers or publishers. Some agents won't read it if the material is with other agents at the same time.

### How to present your submission

It is obvious, but as we receive badly presented material on a regular basis, you should be aware of the following.

- The material must be typed and on one side of the paper only.
- Use double-line spacing with good margins on all four sides.
- Type dialogue and directions correctly. This is particularly important for film and television scripts (each has a different layout that can be checked in most books on screenwriting, also see pp.218–19 for examples of standard TV and screenplay script layouts).
- Be consistent in spelling, headings, paragraph indentation, capitals, etc.
- Read through when finished for spelling and typing mistakes. Show that you care about your work. It really does create a better impression.
- Don't bind, punch, staple or paperclip anything but *do* number the pages. It's a recurring nightmare for some agents and editors

that they will be reading a script or manuscript that will drop on the floor (or in the bath!) before discovering that the pages aren't numbered.

- Make sure your name, address, email and telephone/fax number are featured prominently on the title page.
- By all means put a copyright line (a small 'c' in a circle followed by your name and the year) on the title page but do not put it on every page. That suggests you are paranoid.
- Always include a short synopsis or treatment. This should be more than one paragraph but not more than, say, three pages. At this stage a prospective agent needs to know a little about the subject, characters, period and locations, but do not bore the agent with unnecessary detail.

---

I prefer not to read a script or manuscript until I have read a short synopsis. This helps me determine the genre and whether it is of interest to the agency. From the synopsis and my reading of the opening scenes or chapters I can also usually assess whether the writer has achieved what they set out to achieve.

---

- Do not send random pages from the script or manuscript. (This does happen, really!) A submission of, for example, pages 1, 5, 27, 93, 176 and 206 does not show a writer to their best ability. Do not send chapter one or scene one and then the final chapter or scene. For a TV script always send the whole script.
- Always include a short CV giving the agent some idea of your background. This can influence the decision to see the script or novel.

- Always send a stamped addressed envelope unless it is an emailed submission. Our agency, along with many others, does not return unsolicited material unless there is a SAE.

> Writers should never pay a reading fee to an agency. There are some editorial consultants who, for a fee, will provide an analysis of the project and recommendations to improve it but an agency considering material for representation should not charge to read it.

### Following up

Assume that any good agent is busy. It can take from two weeks to two months for something to be read. In our agency we always read our existing clients' material first. We have over 200 clients, most of whom are working most of the time. This means that there is always material from them arriving to be read. After that has been done, we read the material from prospective clients. Usually this is read in the order in which it is received. We try to be as quick as we can but there are times when a succession of business trips (and even holidays) may mean that there is little time to read. We do not use outside readers because we believe that no one else can tell us if we like the way someone writes. Most agencies do the reading in-house.

Therefore, give your submission at least six to eight weeks before sending a polite reminder and if you must telephone, do not insist on speaking to the agent. Speak to their assistant. If I receive a call from someone chasing me for a response to unsolicited material, all I can do is point out that over the previous four weeks there were several hundred submissions to the agency. Neither I nor my colleagues keep the details in our heads, so we will have to get back to them. By all means leave a message but write rather than ring. We are aware that it must be frustrating to have to wait but we have to prioritise our existing clients.

## Meeting agents

Once you have the interest of an agent, you should meet them. It is important to find out how well you get on with each other. Prepare for the meeting. Think through your career objectives. Read a few books about the business. Read the trade magazines. Make up an agenda so you don't forget anything. Usually an agent will be happy to talk through a career strategy with a new client since it is, after all, in the agent's interest to do so.

If you treat an initial meeting with an agent as an opportunity to gather information, you will benefit even if it doesn't result in your working with that agent. You might gain information on other areas in which you could try writing, such as series and serials (do you watch enough of them?) or whether you should try writing a novel as well as scripts.

From the above you should be able to identify an appropriate agent, submit some material and hope that not only does your writing attract their interest but that they have room for a client like yourself. Don't be surprised if the successful agencies are full. Full doesn't always mean totally full – if an agent finds a writer who is better than one they represent, they may change their minds. They might even have to let one client go in order to make room for a new one. So persevere, write better and more polished scripts, for which you can see there is a market (in terms of genre and format), network in the flesh and on the web – blog and Tweet. You will build a profile and begin to meet agents and increase your chances even when their lists are full.

## The writer-agent relationship

The difficulty in finding an agent tends to make writers anxious to please and they seem to believe that an agent will solve all their problems. This is not true but we will look at some of the main aspects of the relationship here so that you have a broad understanding of the benefits and responsibilities of both parties.

## The author/agency agreement

Writers often ask about the importance of having contracts with their agents. The Association of Authors' Agents (AAA) advises that the business relationship between writer and agent should be formalised in a contract. It's the simplest and most effective way for each party to know the other's obligations and responsibilities.

Below are some of the key points of which you should be aware. These come from the author/agency agreement used by members of the AAA and they are sensible and should be in any good agreement.

1. All approaches regarding your work should be referred to the agent.

2. The agent should not commit you to any agreement without your approval.

3. You should warrant that you are the author and sole owner of the work you ask the agent to represent and that the works are original and contain nothing unlawful in content, do not violate the rights of any third party, are not an infringement of any existing copyright, contain no blasphemous, indecent, defamatory, libellous, objectionable or otherwise unlawful matter, and that all

statements in your work that you say are facts are true. You will also have to indemnify the agent against loss, injury or damage caused by any breach of your warranty. If you have a co-writer, both of you need to make the warranties.

4. The agent's commission should be clearly stated.

5. Should you wish to terminate the representation you should be able to do so at any time. The representation will continue until terminated by either party giving not less than 30 days' written notice to the other. At this point, unless both parties agree otherwise, the agency will cease to represent you but will continue to be entitled to commission in respect of all income arising from existing contracts for the exploitation of your works entered into while they represented you and from all extensions and renewals of such contracts.

## Working with your agent

Agents run businesses and have to make a profit from the 10%–15% of the income earned by their clients (all their overheads have to come out of the commission before there can be a profit). Agents invest time and money when they believe that they (through their clients) will generate a profitable income.

One of the ways agents have of evaluating success is whether they make a sale, and they usually look at scripts with that in mind. It may not matter whether the writing in question is highly-original and complex or a straightforward episode of a long-running series. Advancing the client's career, selling what they have written, collecting the money and deducting the due commission are the core of the agent's functions.

I do not know what our submission-to-sale ratio is but it is not likely to be pretty: the majority of script submissions made by all agents fail. Every agent has stories about selling a script or a book on the twentieth or even thirtieth submission but the average number of submissions per script or novel is probably not far from that. If a script submission isn't sold after a while, it's put on the shelf unless the agent really loves it.

Agents who make submissions that receive negative reactions tend to grin and bear it and get on with the next submission. There is no point in allowing it to become personal or taking each rejection badly. Even if an agent knows they have offered the work to the right person, but that person can't see the merit in it or they want to buy it but can't afford it at that time, an agent has to move on.

Something that hasn't found a buyer may of course still sell. Agents are usually in a better position than writers working on their own to identify potential new buyers. The problem arises when you have tried all the likely outlets but haven't found a buyer. Writers like to think that their agent will continue to go on submitting. The time comes, though, when an agent can't find any serious players who have not seen the script. How far down the list of minor players the agent goes depends on how keen the agent is on the piece of work and on the writer.

Sometimes, if a script is getting a poor reception, an agent may stop submitting it in order to preserve the writer's standing with other companies.

Bear in mind, each submission costs an agency money. The real figure, taking into account the telephone calls, the dictation and typing of the submission letter, the time photocopying, packing and postage (though emailing scripts is far more common now than hard copy submissions), and a portion of overheads of the agency, can be up to £100 per submission.

Eventually, if a script or manuscript has no bites at all – even if it comes close – an agent will stop submitting it. If the writer doesn't agree with this then the writer and agent should talk about it. If they fundamentally disagree, then perhaps the writer should find a new agent. However, it would usually be better for the two of them to work together to develop something else that may have a better chance and then later, if the circumstances change, try to sell the previous piece of work. All that needs to happen is for some of the writer's work to start selling.

All successful writers have scripts that have never sold or, if they were optioned, have not been produced. Don't wait until a script fails to sell: once you have delivered the polished draft to your agent you should be working on something new, preferably having discussed your choice or preference with your agent. You should be a team.

The relationship between agent and client can encompass editorial work, a shoulder to cry on, a business adviser and career manager. At Blake Friedmann we suggest ideas and storylines that we believe we can sell and which we think a particular writer can execute really well if they do not have equally good ideas of their own. We read the drafts and provide some quality control (though we are not really editors in the full sense of the word, except in exceptional cases, because it is very time consuming).

However, there are two parties to the relationship and like any relationship this one needs nurturing and each writer and agent is unique. So develop the relationship as you would any professional one, with respect and transparency and openness.

Agents need to be realistic, to counter the healthy optimism of some clients who think that what they have written is almost always wonderful. They also need to be able to enthuse about the good work done by clients who have little confidence. Sometimes agents need to bring the cold light of reality to bear on a piece of writing. If the agent is good at his or her job, they will not allow their clients to 'die of encouragement', as Pauline Kael once put it.

## The key tasks of the agent

- Find work for writers, know market prices, negotiate contracts.
- Guide the writer's career.
- Work with producers to raise the finance for client-written projects.
- Evaluate material coming in from clients and work with them on treatments and scripts so that producers may assume that if a script or novel is agented, it is saleable.
- Try to select successful writers: no sale, no commission to the agent.
- See both points of view in any situation – the producer's and the writer's – but always do their best for the client. An agent's reputation depends on being trusted. We are in a long-term business, otherwise known as 'repeat' business, which means it becomes more profitable if we are able to sell more than once to the same producer.
- Do more development work than most script editors or development executives.

This no doubt sounds great for those with an agent but you need to be able to be your own agent until you get one and once you have one, you need to know exactly what the agent's responsibilities are.

## *The legal responsibilities of the agent*

An agent has certain obligations to clients in common law. These can be summed up as follows (this is not an exhaustive list).

- An agent has legal and fiduciary obligations to clients.
- The rights and duties of the principal (i.e. the writer) and the agent are to be determined in a contract between them. If there is no contract, the fact that the relationship exists implies a contract.
- The primary duty of an agent is to carry out the business the agent has undertaken with the principal and to notify the principal if he or she is unable to do it.
- The agent must always act in the best interests of a client. The agent must either follow the client's instructions or if it is not possible to obtain instructions, the interests of the client must guide the agent's actions.
- There is an obligation on the agent to keep proper accounts and to disclose them on reasonable demand to the client.
- The agent is obliged to disclose any conflict of interests. This means the agent can't be paid by both the producer and the writer.
- The agent must disclose any information gathered by the agency that is relevant to the client's interests.
- The agent must not receive any secret commission or bribe with regard to a client's contracts.
- The agent should not commit the client unless the agent has general or specific authority to do so.
- An agent should exercise skill, care and diligence in what they undertake to do on behalf of clients.

> The writer-agent relationship is exclusive – a writer should
> not have more than one agent in a territory selling the
> same rights though some do have separate US and UK
> agents, and some have a book agent and a script agent in
> the same country.

## The writer's responsibilities

Like any relationship, what you put in relates to what you derive so
any assessment of the agent's responsibilities needs a comment on
the writer's responsibilities.

An agent can only work with material supplied by the writer; this is
why writers need to be constantly working on new ideas, treatments
and scripts (in consultation with the agent). A writer should not
surprise their agent with a completed draft of a script that has not
been discussed beforehand.

An agent's responsibilities also include telling the truth when a
script isn't good enough. Whether that script should be submitted
is a matter of risk-judgement that should be discussed. Send out a
bad calling card script and the writer will almost certainly not be
added to the database of the production company as someone they
should keep an eye on when they need a writer. (They all keep data-
bases like this.) If selling that early draft script is the main agenda,
however, then submitting it, saying that the writer wants to do more
work on it with an interested producer, can lead to an option deal.

It is important for writers to understand why an agent suggests
certain courses of action rather than others. Listen to the advice
given. You presumably listen to advice from your accountant or
dentist. If you do not agree with it, say so but do not dismiss it out

of hand. Rather, 'I'm not sure I agree but I will think about it carefully,' or 'That's interesting. I will think it over'.

If an agent suggests revisions, remember that they will have spent their own time and money reading your work. They will only suggest those revisions if they think the script or manuscript will benefit. The revisions will also have been suggested with knowledge of the industry and the marketplace, not with the intention of interfering with your work.

Sometimes writers have agendas that they haven't discussed with their agents. This may be because the writer does not really know why he or she is writing or what their priorities should be. If a client says, 'I need as much cash as fast as possible,' then the agent can try to achieve that (even though it could lead to an overall lousy deal) in order to maximise the cash up front payment. In general, to maximise the financial return, a writer may need to be prepared for it to take longer to establish a deal. This is obviously also true if you are selling your own work.

It does not matter whether the agent found the buyer or the buyer found the writer or the piece of work. Agents are not paid their commission only because they find the buyer. If writers want to pay less because they – the writer – find the buyer, then they ought to be prepared to pay some of the costs incurred in the submissions that do not result in a sale.

What agents lose on the submissions that don't attract deals, they have to make up on the sales. Agents should represent 'writers' not scripts or manuscripts. The career of the client should be uppermost in the agent's mind, not just any quick deal to keep the client happy today.

The work of an agent therefore encompasses far more than doing deals. In our agency we spend a great deal of time on creative editorial work. This is partly because we enjoy it but mainly because we recognise that it makes money. At the end of the day, whatever the writer's motivations are for writing (and agents may share some of the more personal and subjective ones) most agents run businesses in order to make money.

You should remember that to use your agent properly you need to keep them well briefed. This means the agent should hear from the writer, not from the producer or publisher, when things are going wrong or if deadlines will not be met.

You should not make the mistake of allowing the producer or broadcaster to get between you and your agent. The agent and writer should work as a team and there should be room for healthy disagreement on both creative and business matters. Disagreement can be constructive and your agent will be on your side far more often than on your producer's or publisher's side. When it is the latter, there is probably a good reason for it and you should consider your agent's advice carefully. You, though, are the principal so it is up to you whether or not to accept advice or a deal.

It is very helpful when pitching a writer for an agent to be able to say that the client is working on something that is going into production or that a client is writing a script for a producer of some stature. We might, therefore, sometimes encourage a client to take a deal that may not be as good as they or we would like because it will open up other avenues for them. This is always discussed.

That is the way the business actually works. Just sending out material that may not be ready or appropriate is a fairly thankless task. It helps when a writer acquires a good reputation and producers ring up and ask to see their work, which is why I emphasise so strongly the importance of building your reputation and developing your knowledge of the industry. It will pay off and is often the way that less talented writers get more work than talented writers.

Strategy and tactics should always be discussed between agent and client. We never mind spending time with a client explaining why we think they should do something or why we are following a particular route with their work. They may disagree with us. If we think that their decision will be damaging to their career and reputation, we may choose not to go on working with them. After all, we also have careers and reputations to worry about. However, if a good agent is discouraging about a particular storyline or about the way it has been written, it may mean that it is not good enough.

> Be wary of listening only to what you want to hear. Seek criticism and always try to improve your work because with that frame of mind you are more likely to attract an agent, if you also write well enough . . .

When an agented writer is approached directly by a producer, script editor or publisher, the writer should report back to the agent, who may have background knowledge of the producer that the writer does not know. You should always tell them that you are represented by an agent.

Smaller and newer producers seldom have much money. They should know that for an agent to draw up a contract will cost the agent money. So why would an agent want to do a deal with little or no money involved? They don't. It is as simple as that. Agents do it, however, because they and their clients mutually agree it is a risk worth taking and an investment worth making.

In the working relationship with an agent, try to acquire advice on how you should establish a price for your work and your time. If a producer asks you out of the blue what you will charge for writing something, you should either have a good idea or graciously ask the producer to talk to your agent about it. It is perfectly acceptable for a writer to say that they never discuss money.

However good your relationship with your agent, be considerate of his or her time. If you need information from the agency, think about who else there is on the staff who can give it to you more easily. I don't appreciate authors who ring me to ask for a copy of their contract or last royalty statement. They should talk to the agency's finance director who, they know, takes care of that side of the business. I should be trying to make money, if not for that writer, then for another. A successful agency generally benefits all its clients. We tell all new clients who in the agency has what responsibility. All members of staff are listed in the author/agency letter we sign with our clients. If your agency doesn't give you this information, you should ask for it.

One final thought about how to use agents: after deals are agreed and contracts concluded and signed, some agents don't send signed copies of their clients' contracts to them. You should always keep a copy for your own files. This helps you (or your accountant) to keep track of finances and sort out your taxes (as long as you also keep all royalty statements or other documentation). It is also the only way you will be able to brief your new agent should you want to change agents or your estate can find out what your assets are should you die.

## Firing your agent

If you are thinking of changing agent you can certainly start talking to new agents before you break the news to your existing one. All agents, in my experience, treat such conversations in confidence. (If an agency became known for not respecting their clients' confidentiality, they would find it hard to attract new clients.)

So, if it makes you feel more secure, interview several other agents first. Tell them you are represented but that you want to move.

You may decide to leave because you are approached by another agent. Sometimes they do so because they have read something you have written and like it. They may not necessarily know you have an agent.

If you begin to feel that your agent is doing nothing for your career, it will rapidly undermine the relationship. Whatever the cause, if your relationship is not that good, this might be a good moment to leave. Talk to your existing agent first. Express your feelings and make your leaving as businesslike and unacrimonious as possible. They are still the agent of record for your past contracts; you need them to cooperate with your new agent. The new agent should request sight of all your contracts and should arrange to collect and copy them before returning them to your ex-agent. You may have copies of them yourself, which would speed up this process.

> You will not be the first writer to fire an agent. Don't worry too much about it. Just do it sensibly and constructively. You and your agent will survive.

If you are fired, do some research into alternative agents, talk to writer friends, to producers and script editors. Get recommendations. You do not need to admit you were fired: you could instead indicate that there had been a difference of opinion about your direction for example (but be prepared to explain it) that made you feel you needed a change. Send in a letter with your CV and a couple of samples. Make the agent feel that you are ambitious, hard working, and take advice.

So how do you fire your agent? Easy. Look at the agreement you have signed. If there is a 30-day notice period then write a letter giving the agent notice. If you do not have a written agreement with your agent, write to them informing them that you are withdrawing from them the right to represent you. You can make this immediate but it will be better all-round if you make it 30 days, allowing the agent to receive any answers and offers from submissions already made.

You have the right to accept or reject such offers. If you accept an offer made in this period, the agent becomes the 'agent of record' for that deal and they negotiate the contract and collect the money, remitting to you less the agreed commission, for the duration of the life of that contract. It is important that you keep clear the fact that you are the principal. *You* will sign the contract, not your agent.

Unless you have inadvisably signed a contract that commits you for a period longer than the 30 days' notice, you are free to fire your agent when you choose. You may feel nervous about doing this. This is natural. Most people do not like firing others, especially if there is still a continuing relationship. It is your career and you must put yourself first, before your agent.

The most common misunderstanding in firing agents seems to be the question of whether the agent is entitled to continue to collect commission on monies coming in from earlier contracts.

Unless there is something written and signed to the contrary, the 'agent of record' (i.e. the agent who handled the contract) is entitled to commission on all revenues from that contract during its life.

If, after an agent has been fired, the contract, say for a licence to publish a book or for the rights in a script, should terminate, then the owner of the rights – the writer – is free to move that contract away from that agent.

Whether or not your representation contract gives the agent the protection of 30 days to collect offers from submissions already made, you can instruct them not to make any more submissions. You can also refuse to accept any offers that the agent brings in after they have been fired (i.e. in the 30-day period).

However, if there are live contracts that the agent will be handling on your behalf, it makes sense to suggest an amicable separation. If this is not possible, you can instruct the producer or publisher to pay the monies due directly to you, rather than to your ex-agent, less the agent's commission, which should be paid directly to the agent.

## Doing without an agent

Acting as your own agent is difficult: it is difficult if you know few people in the business and don't network. It is difficult if you don't have a clue what the contracts should include or how to work out what money you should be paid. It is difficult if you are a shy retiring sort who hates self-promotion. And it is difficult if the company you want to submit to insists that they will only accept submissions from an agent.

One way to overcome the last obstacle mentioned is to win script-writing competitions, so go online and be bemused by how many there are, both in the UK and especially in the USA. See Chapter 4 for more information on competitions.

Go to the PACT website and peruse their membership list. This will give you many leads as to whom you should submit your work to. Make a note of the credits in shows you see on movies to build up your own list of companies to approach and read the trade papers regularly.

Get to know your screen agency: there is Creative England, Creative Scotland, Creative Wales and Creative Northern Ireland. These are the organisations which are being provided with funding from the British Film Institute (www.bfi.org.uk), so start by looking at their website. Also go to the Edinburgh Film and Television Festival (www.edfilmfest.org.uk), the London Screenwriters' Festival (www.londonscreenwritersfestival.com) and any other major venues where professional writers and producers are in attendance. Check the EU media desks in your country and also the Skillset website (www.skillset.org).

Have your pitches prepared to perfection so that in less than 60 seconds you can pitch whichever of your projects seems most appropriate.

Keep meticulous records of every submission (a pitch at a cocktail party which is rejected is a failed submission so enter that in your record book).

Be careful submitting to broadcasters since if you are rejected by them, you really have to tell an independent producer you later submit to, who is then unlikely to commit to your project.

Remember that producers are more likely to want writers for projects they are more or less committed to, rather than wanting to buy your spec work.

Have a simple, elegant business card ready to offer and follow up every meeting with a friendly email, even if all you are doing is thanking someone for their time.

If you know you are going to meet a producer (maybe they are on a seminar panel) then research their work and be ready to ask a question that shows you know what they have done and, if possible, say something nice (without seeming too smarmy).

Read the trade papers carefully so you can talk to producers about the world as they see it. Do you know what the criteria are for a qualifying British film or where there are new co-production treaties? Probably not. That will make it difficult for you to impress a producer (or agent) who may not have read your script and might be thinking that they need a new spec script like the proverbial hole in the head.

In other words, there are many things you can do to help yourself – the wonder is that so few writers do them – which means if you do, you will be at an advantage over your competition.

## A final word about the writer-agent relationship

Good agents look for long-term relationships with their clients. How much a client earns for an agent in a given period of time is not the only factor the agent takes into account, especially if the agent believes in a client's abilities and shares the determination to make a success of the client's work.

There are many instances when agents have worked with writers for years before either made significant money out of the arrangement. Unfortunately, there are also cases where a suddenly successful author feels that they have become too big for their agency and, because of the success gained with the agency, they leave.

What is clear is that the relationship is most effective if there is mutual respect. It should be a team effort and when it works, it is extremely rewarding. Never forget, though, that your writing career is the only one you have. The agent has other clients.

## The business of being a television writer

From development hell to being a credited and produced television writer can be only a few steps, or it can take years. Training, networking with industry players, offering well-written scripts in carefully-chosen subjects or in carefully-chosen genres, can make all the difference between a career or not, as long as you have the craft skills to match your business acumen and preparation.

In the next part of this book we will provide a comprehensive and practical guide to the craft skills you need to be a successful television writer.

# The art and craft of writing for television audiences

# 10 What do audiences watch?

'I thought drama was when actors cried. But drama is when the audience cries.'

*Frank Capra, director of* It's a Wonderful Life

In other words, it's not what is happening on the screen that is the key to successful drama, but how it affects the audience. Writing for television is about understanding, reaching, engaging and holding that audience and this part of the book focuses on how to do that.

If you want to write for television audiences, then you need to study what programmes audiences are watching (the ratings), where they are watching (the channels) and when they are watching (the schedule). Analyse why particular programmes succeed and others fail and learn from others' experience. This is the world you are planning to enter and you need to be very familiar with it, not only to help you decide what to write, but also to give you credibility when you start to talk to people in the business.

## The importance of ratings

Anybody interested in writing for television needs to be aware of what audiences are watching, even if they are not watching those particular programmes themselves. The ratings are published in *Broadcast* every week. As well as the top 100 network programmes, there are individual genre top tens (drama, comedy, children's etc.)

across all channels. In addition to the numbers of viewers, the share of the audience is also published, i.e. the programme's share of all the people watching television at that time. Although there will be seasonal variations in the actual size of audiences, the share should not be affected and is constantly monitored.

Ratings, or in some cases the right kind of demographics, are what all broadcasters are most concerned about. This is understandable in the case of commercial broadcasters, who only survive by delivering audiences to advertisers, but even the BBC is not immune from this preoccupation with ratings. Programmes will only be commissioned if there is sufficient confidence that they will deliver a sizeable audience. Programmes will only be re-commissioned if they have achieved appropriate ratings. A few years ago good reviews and a positive industry response might have been enough to earn a low-rating series a second chance (e.g. *Footballers' Wives*), but commercial pressures today are less forgiving.

### *BARB*

BARB (Broadcasters Audience Research Board) is the main provider of television audience measurement in the UK. It is a non-profit making limited company, funded by the major players in the industry it supports, namely the BBC, ITV, Channel 4, Five, BSkyB and the IPA (Institute of Practitioners in Advertising). It covers all channels broadcasting across all platforms – terrestrial, satellite and cable. The data provided by BARB underpins the trading currency for broadcasters, advertisers and their agencies. It enables broadcasters to define success and determines how much advertisers should pay.

## The multi-channel environment

According to BARB, 2.3 million homes had access to non-terrestrial channels in 1992. By January 2010 that figure had risen to 23.8 million. The free to air DTT Freeview platform has been very influential in this process, currently providing viewers with around 50 channels without a subscription. BARB now reports on 290 UK channels across all platforms. In spite of the popularity of alternative screens (PCs, laptops, iPhones etc.), increased choice has in fact had a positive effect on traditional TV consumption. The average daily TV viewing time per person is increasing: from 218 minutes in 2007 to 243 minutes in 2011.

In 1997 the collective share of viewing of the non-terrestrial channels was 10.1%, while BBC1 had 30.8% and ITV1 32.9%. By 2009 that collective share had risen to 41.4% and BBC1 and ITV1 had decreased to 20.9% and 17.8% respectively. This adverse affect on the mainstream channels, who are the principal commissioners, has had serious implications for original programme making and in turn for writers.

To stabilise viewing share, traditional broadcasters are having to broaden and diversify their offerings to the audience:

- by providing complementary digital channels (e.g. BBC3, ITV2, E4 etc.) to expand and enforce the brand and offer increased viewer choice within the brand
- through '+1' time shift channels
- through online seven-day video on demand catch-up services (e.g. BBC iPlayer, ITV Player, 4 on Demand etc.).

The success of ITV2, ITV3 and ITV4 has helped ITV offset the decline of ITV1's viewing share, by targeting specific audience segments:

- ITV2 'a fun-loving, brand conscious, younger audience of 16–34s with a female bias'
- ITV3 'a channel for sophisticated, upmarket audiences, full of character-driven narrative and drama that stirs the emotions'
- ITV4 'brings quality entertainment to men with a core audience of 25–44 year old males including comedy, cult classics, movies and sport'.

(*Source: ITV Media website*)

Its suite of channels allows ITV to make claims about the breadth of its overall audience reach that would be impossible with the relatively older skewing ITV1 alone.

In a similar way the BBC and Channel 4 have developed their own channels. While BBC2's 'key focus is to appeal to a heartland of viewers aged 35–54', BBC3's 'centre of gravity will be 16–34 year olds: people who are young in spirit and mindset', and BBC4 is an 'intelligent' channel with an audience for whom 'television must compete with radio, books, print journalism, online and digital media, and a host of interests and passions'. (BBC Commissioning website). Channel 4's E4 'is the UK's most-watched digital channel amongst 16–34 year olds' (Channel 4 Commissioning website). Its comedy series *The Inbetweeners* had an audience of 3.7 million in October 2010 which was enough to make it the ninth most watched sitcom on all channels during a 12-month period.

The success of *The Inbetweeners* on E4 and *Being Human* on BBC3 demonstrates that programmes targeted at niche audiences on more specialised channels can be extremely profitable – it is not simply a case of appealing to as large an audience as possible – and writers can benefit from this more varied television landscape and tailor their ideas accordingly.

## The schedule

Writers need to be aware when particular programmes are scheduled. The most important element of any schedule is the 9pm watershed. This applies to all channels, including cable and satellite, and ensures that no programme that is unsuitable for children, (with particular emphasis on violence, sex and swearing), is broadcast before this time. BBC1 and ITV1 currently have their main news bulletins at 10pm, which makes the scheduling of feature films or any post-watershed drama longer than an hour difficult. Films are often shown around the news, which is not very satisfactory as a two-hour film is not going to finish until after 11.30pm, and this needs to be borne in mind by any writer thinking of submitting a long post-watershed drama to these channels. It might be better to consider tailoring it for BBC2 or Channel 4.

Certain slots in the schedule are well established and audiences will expect to find a specific kind of programming 'brand' there – for instance the pre-watershed Sunday evening drama. From *Doctor Finlay's Casebook* and *All Creatures Great and Small* to *Heartbeat* and *Lark Rise to Candleford*, audiences have warmed to – and continue to be warmed by – cosy, nostalgic, period, invariably rural, long-running series. Nothing too demanding or disturbing on the night before the working week begins. Other slots are more subject to the vagaries of fashion. Until recently there was no demand for early Saturday evening, tea-time drama for the whole family. *Dixon of Dock Green* and *Doctor Who* had been consigned to history and it was received opinion that there was no such thing as a family audience any more. The spectacular success of the revived *Doctor Who* in 2005 disproved this theory and created a new demand for family drama. *Robin Hood* and more recently *Merlin* have filled the *Doctor Who* slot and have also demonstrated that the action adventure genre, long neglected by British TV, is alive and well. The last episode of the third series of *Merlin*, even though it was scheduled against *The X Factor*, was the most popular non-soap drama of the week with an audience of 6.61 million in a drama slot that didn't exist a few years earlier.

Schedules have very specific slot lengths and writers need to be aware of them before deciding how and at what length to tell their story. The customary lengths are:

- 90 minutes – one-off TV movies and occasionally first episodes of drama series
- 60 minutes – most drama series and serials
- 45 minutes – some children's and daytime drama
- 30 minutes – situation comedy and comedy series. Apart from the soaps, there are few if any drama series of this length.

There is no point producing a script of the wrong length for a slot that doesn't exist. The script will have no future, however good it may be, and will not inspire confidence in the reader that you have done your homework and are serious about breaking into the industry.

### Tailoring a show to a slot

Although it is not necessarily a good idea to create a show for a particular slot, it is advisable while you are developing a project to have some idea where it might be placed in the schedule. It will make a project more marketable if a broadcaster can see a potential audience for it and an awareness of that audience will help you to maximise its chances of success. Whether or not you consider it to be a pre-watershed programme will affect the content and tone. Where it is most likely to find a home – in terms of the channel as well as its likely slot in the schedule – will have an effect on the budget, which will impact on what is affordable in terms of number of sets or characters, action sequences or special effects.

*Merlin* is a very good example of a successful show that was carefully tailored to its slot and its budget. A fantasy series with a young magician as its central character has the built-in disadvantage of being very expensive to produce, as magic convincing enough for an audience accustomed to the *Harry Potter* films is going to require a lot of costly and time-consuming special effects. To overcome this problem, the creators of *Merlin* came up with an imaginative solution. When the young Merlin arrives in Camelot he discovers that the king, Uther Pendragon, has outlawed magic. Thus, he has to keep his magic a secret or face execution. Not only does this add a powerful ever-present element of jeopardy for its hero, but it limits the amount of actual magic required in the story! Making magic a capital offence in Camelot keeps *Merlin* within a viable budget and at the same time gives the series a unique twist that makes it different from previous versions of the Arthurian legend.

## What makes a successful TV show? Is there a formula for success?

In *Adventures in the Screen Trade*, Hollywood screenwriter William Goldman famously wrote that 'Nobody knows anything' when it comes to predicting whether or not a script that is commissioned or developed or made is going to be successful. However, as John Peek, director of TAPE (Television Audience Programme Evaluation) Consultancy, points out:

'Audiences *know* what they like: shows that get it right deliver ratings and travel round the world; movies that get it right fill theatres.'

TAPE is a UK-based consultancy company that over 30 years has developed its own system for assessing the 'potential audience return' of programme proposals or scripts or pilots. Based on many years of programme performance study, TAPE's system has identified key elements which appear continually to influence audience choice. By breaking programmes down into their component 'factors' and assessing each element separately, TAPE provides its clients (broadcasters and production companies) with an indication of their 'intrinsic' appeal. Here we look at these factors and how writers should consider their impact on a programme's appeal.

### Characters and relationships

A number of different factors are examined and assessed by TAPE's system, but significantly more than 50% of them relate to the characters. Character accessibility, personality and motivation, as well as the primary and secondary characterisation are all considered. TV shows that fail invariably have problems with the characters and the characterisation. TV shows that succeed consistently have accessible, appealing and engaging characters. If you get the character mix right, you are more than halfway there.

Who the characters are and how they relate to others will always be more important than what they do, although the individual elements can never be totally divorced from one another.

### Relatable characters

In terms of character types, it is clear that audiences prefer ordinary people that they can to some degree identify with as the principals in their dramas. They can be put into extraordinary situations where they are forced to react in a different way to their everyday lives, but at the end of the day they remain 'people like us' rather than super-heroic or larger-than-life characters. The continuing ratings success of the soaps highlights that the everyday events of families and individuals simply living life still holds greater appeal than any other genre of drama.

Even in series based around action rather than human drama, it is essential to get the characters right. The level of action will never be enough if the audience has no affinity with the characters. *24* was built on an original concept and has delivered more thrills per episode than most series, but it would not have lasted eight seasons without Jack Bauer at its centre.

### Camaraderie

A strong element of camaraderie at the core of a relationship will always be a positive element in generating audience appeal.

> 'Merlin is successful because it is a show with tremendous heart. It is the warmth of the relationships – Merlin/Gaius and Merlin/Arthur – that connects with audiences here and all over the world.'
>
> *Julian Jones, co-creator and writer of Merlin*

While conflict is an integral part of character relationships in any type of drama series, it can work against the acceptance of a concept. Too much antagonism between central characters in a series can render them less acceptable to an audience and create an impression of bitterness and aggravation.

### Identifiability

TAPE also stresses the importance of identifiability for an audience. This does not simply mean the depiction of homes, jobs or streets that are familiar to the TV audience, although in many types of drama these are important for reinforcing the credibility of the characters and of the story. Identifiability also extends into the area of motivation and emotions.

While it could be argued that the characters and situations in a *Dallas* or a *Downton Abbey* are not immediately recognisable, the motivation is invariably through factors like love, conflict, ambition etc., which are easily identified with and, indeed, are just as important in *Coronation Street* or *EastEnders*, although not on quite such a 'grand' scale.

What *drives* characters is also an important factor. Not just the emotional aspects, but whether the principal motivation is to help others or to achieve some form of personal satisfaction in terms of wealth or power. These are key elements in the audience's perception of both a character and a series as a whole.

*Cutting It* was a successful series about ambitious and driven women. In a *South Bank Show* interview, Debbie Horsfield, its creator, said:

> 'If they were just ambitious and driven, I don't think anybody would be interested, they'd be completely turned off. I know I would be. But because that is just masking these fragilities and vulnerabilities, which we absolutely see, then we kind of understand what that drive is about and it's not just about "I want to tread on everybody to get to the top". It's because of other weaknesses as well and I think that's what people relate to and that's what they like.'

Ruthless characters need redeeming features, if audiences are going to warm to them.

Although *Downton Abbey* is a notable exception, TAPE maintains that in any comparative situation a concept that is contemporary starts off with an immediate advantage. It is inevitable that the audience will prefer their own time and equally the preference will also be for the domestic setting as opposed to any overseas location.

While the UK audience is not as resistant to foreign settings and characters as the American audience, it remains a fact that most projects that are not set in Britain will have a potential built-in disadvantage that will require strengths elsewhere to offset.

*Death in Paradise*, a well-crafted murder mystery series, makes a virtue of its setting on an exotic Caribbean island. Not only do the 'blue skies' provide 'wish you were there' escapism for UK audiences during autumn and winter, but the slow pace of life and limited access to modern technology mean that the detective stories inhabit very familiar Agatha Christie territory, but with a modern slant. Grumpy DI Richard Poole's dislike of sun and heat, which plays against the tropical setting, is all part of the fun.

TAPE notes that the central theme of a show is very clearly linked with the whole area of identifiability. Although few members of the audience will have any idea of what it is really like to be involved in a police raid or experience the type of powerful family relationships and emotions depicted in many drama series, they nonetheless know of these things and regard them as credible.

The further a theme gets away from this sort of identifiability and credibility, the more difficult it seems to become to generate a viable degree of audience involvement that will boost a series' potential for an extended run. This normally indicates an audience preference for the straightforward – action where it is quite clear who the heroes are and what they do; dramas featuring families 'in sickness and in health' or groups of characters in some form of escapist or dramatic situations that tell a good story in clear narrative style.

### External factors

External factors – whether they are social, psychological, political, economic, or even seasonal – can all have an influence on the viewing decision, which in itself is mostly subconscious and instinctive. As *Downton Abbey* clearly demonstrates, period/nostalgia provides an escape from the grim economic reality of current times – when things were more ordered or simpler (or at least perceived to be). It also has a fantastic visual look, which cements that feeling of escape. It is also a cultural phenomenon, in that UK audiences are more willing to accept period drama (done well) than their American counterparts.

At present comedy is on an upturn for much the same reason – especially in the USA, and especially revolving round friends and family – the core values people fall back on in times of difficulty. So contemporary takes on traditional family scenarios – such as *Modern Family* – are doing well, as are dramas dealing with contemporary family realities in lighter ways – e.g. the Australian drama *Packed to the Rafters* (about adult children moving back home), which has quickly become one of Australia's most successful dramas ever. Even the extreme take of Channel 4's only truly successful drama *Shameless*, of which a re-formatted version has launched successfully on Showtime in the USA, follows this model.

Pure fantasy is also proving more successful now than in the past as a result of the audience's desire to escape – which has aided series like *Merlin*, as well as imports such as *Glee* (a rare example of a TV musical drama that has sustained appeal). There are clear echoes here of the huge popularity of Hollywood musicals in the 1930s. However, there are limits – which is arguably illustrated by the BBC's *Outcasts*: earth-bound science fiction can deliver in broad, mainstream terms, but stray further afield and there is a very real danger of rejection, because the themes and situations explored are much harder to relate to. Regardless of any external factors, identifiability for an audience remains crucial.

*Outcasts*, a 'blockbuster sci-fi series' (BBC Press Pack), was about a group of pioneers given 'the chance to build a new and better future on another planet'. Commissioned in 2007 from Kudos Film and Television, the company responsible for *Life on Mars* and *Spooks*, and filmed in South Africa, the BBC had high hopes for this eight-part series when it was launched in February 2011. However, initial viewing figures were disappointing and the reviews were mainly hostile. As audiences declined, the show was moved from 9pm on a Monday to a Sunday late-night slot. It did not return for a second series.

# 11 What audiences want

Lord Reith, the founder of the BBC, set out to educate, inform and entertain. Education and information are still there in the broadcasting mix, but overwhelmingly what a television audience wants is to be entertained. The most entertaining programmes, whether drama or entertainment or live sport, are inevitably the most emotionally involving. Emotional involvement comes from connecting with appealing characters engaged in strong stories – whether that is Jack Bauer in *24*, Susan Boyle in *Britain's Got Talent* or Goran Ivanisevic finally winning Wimbledon.

The appeal of ratings blockbusters like *The X Factor*, *I'm a Celebrity* or *The Apprentice* stems from the narrative arc of each series, in which the characters (each with their loyal fans) compete to be the last one standing and to achieve their goal. These shows, like *Big Brother*, are built on the principle of a balloon debate, in which the participants have to convince their audience not to vote them off.

Speaking at the inaugural London Screenwriters' Festival, Ben Stephenson, BBC Controller, Drama Commissioning, said:

'Connecting with the audience is what we do.'

Writing for television is all about connecting with the audience.

What does the audience want?

- **stories**
- **characters**
- **emotions**.

In this chapter we will look at how to get the story right.

## What's the story?

Before you start writing, you need to determine whether your story is strong enough. In simple terms – is there enough in it to engage and hold an audience?

Consider the following questions:

- whose story is it?
- what are they trying to achieve?
- what's stopping them from achieving it?
- what's at stake?
- do they get what they want?
- how are they affected by the experience?

These are questions which any writer should ask of any story to ensure it is one which will emotionally appeal to the audience.

### Whose story is it?

Although there may be a number of characters in your story, you have to decide which character to focus on and from whose perspective the story will be told – the protagonist. This is the character that the audience will relate to and the character they will be rooting for. If the story lacks this focus, there is a danger that the audience will remain uninvolved and that the script will seem confused. There may be subplots, but a cinema film or television single drama will conventionally have one main storyline. However, in an episode of a television series, it is likely that there will be a number of different storylines that are woven together. Nevertheless, each of these storylines will have its own *protagonist*, as these TV listings demonstrate.

*Coronation Street:* **Gail** urges Audrey not to sign over the salon to David, **Jim** faces a setback with his plans for the pub, and **Graeme** has a rendezvous with Tina.

*Holby City:* **Sahira's** judgement is tested on the day of the consultancy interviews, and **Malick** suppresses his aggression while dealing with a stab wound.

*Hollyoaks:* A visit from Ste prompts **Cheryl** to see Brendan in a new light, **Rhys** tries to make his feelings known, and **Riley** comes into conflict with Warren.

(*Daily Mail Weekend*, 2 April 2011)

### What are they trying to achieve?

The goal of the protagonist is the point of a story. This is what the story is about. Something happens, which throws that character's life out of balance. Robert McKee, in his 'story' seminars, calls this the inciting incident; others refer to it as the point of attack, the call to adventure or the hook. It is this moment that creates the character's *want*. Their want, their goal, their quest is whatever it is that they feel will put their life back in balance. However, characters with any depth will also have an underlying *need* (which may be different from their want), which will motivate their actions. In *Prime Suspect VII: The Final Act*, Jane Tennison 'wants' to find the murderer of a missing schoolgirl and to solve her final case, but she 'needs' to face up to her alcohol problem and to pull herself together in order to do so.

In order to achieve their goal your character has to go on a journey. The journey can be an internal or an external one, but it is essential that the character doesn't simply stay where they are. The story must end up in a different place from where it started. In some stories that may physically be the same place, but like Dorothy in *The Wizard of Oz*, the characters will look at their world differently at the end of their journey. The character's journey does not necessarily have to be a very long one; in an episode of a television series it probably won't be, compared to the central character in a film, but a small step can still be significant. A story without a character journey is not going anywhere.

---

## The character's journey

Based on his studies of the myths and legends of different cultures, Joseph Campbell outlined the archetypal hero's journey in *The Hero with a Thousand Faces*, demonstrating that all stories conform to a particular pattern. George Lucas drew heavily on Campbell's work when he was creating *Star Wars*, a modern fairytale, and brought him to the attention of other film-makers and scriptwriters. In *The Writer's Journey: Mythic Structure for Storytellers and Screenwriters*, Christopher Vogler describes how Campbell's work can help screenwriters shape their stories and discusses the significance and relevance of each stage of the hero's journey.

---

### What's stopping them from achieving it?

There may be another character (the antagonist), who is blocking the protagonist's path, the circumstances in which they find themselves or, indeed, flaws in their own character that are holding them back. Whatever or whoever the forces of antagonism may be, it is essential that there are sufficient obstacles that have to be overcome to make for compelling drama. There is no drama without conflict and the more challenging the obstacles, the more gripping the drama.

### What's at stake?

If the character doesn't reach their goal, what are the consequences? It may be loss of face, death or even the destruction of the planet. Always ensure that what is at stake is appropriate for the kind of script you are writing – don't have the reputation of a quiz expert at risk in an episode of *24* or the world at risk in an episode of *The Office*. Clearly the higher the stakes, the better. A story where very little is at stake is not a story that is going to involve an audience.

### Do they get what they want?

How does the story end? Is this a satisfactory conclusion for the audience? Is it credible? You need to consider how you want the audience to feel at the end. Not only will the ending dictate the way in which the story is told, but different audiences will have different expectations. Most mainstream television drama is reassuring and the audience will demand a positive outcome. Edgier drama can deliver more challenging and disturbing denouements.

### How are they affected by the experience?

It is important that characters are affected by the experience of their journey and learn something from it. Stories that have no impact on the characters are not going to have any impact on the audience. Films are always about characters who change – with the exception of action heroes like James Bond or Rambo, who are always the same. It is the change in the characters, often by the discovery of their true nature through the choices they make, which delivers the emotional impact to the audience. Characters in television series, particularly situation comedies, tend to stay the same. Nevertheless, they will still learn something from their experience, even if they have forgotten it in time for the next episode!

## Structure

When you are sure you have a viable story, you need to decide how you are going to tell it. Audiences have always responded to stories being told in a certain way. Writers follow these established patterns, because they know they work. Remember the films or TV shows that have really gripped or moved you. As a writer you can draw on your own experience as an audience member to help you to shape your own stories most effectively. How should you start? How should you end? How should you get there? Close attention needs to be paid to the structure of your script, once you have a firm foundation (a great story) to build it on.

### The three act structure

The three act structure is the basis of most dramatic storytelling. Every story has a beginning, a middle and an end or, in the case of many television sitcoms, a beginning, a muddle and an end. In Act One, we are introduced to the protagonist, a problem occurs and they resolve to do something about it. At the same time the antagonist and/or the forces of antagonism are also established. In Act Two (where the bulk of the dramatic action occurs), various obstacles have to be overcome, often with varied degrees of success, as the protagonist strives to achieve their goal. In Act Three, everything is brought to a dramatic climax and the initial problem is or is not solved and the protagonist achieves or does not achieve their goal. In any event, there is some kind of resolution.

Although this three act structure underpins television drama, the way in which television is presented means that this structure often has to be adapted and subdivided. A commercial television half-hour slot has a break in the middle, so there are effectively two acts. A commercial television hour slot has four breaks, so there are five acts. Because of these breaks, a BBC half-hour or one-hour slot contains considerably more screen time than its commercial equivalent and writers need to be aware of this when developing a script for a specific broadcaster. Experienced ITV drama writers have often found it a challenge when writing a BBC hour for the first time and having to produce almost 10 minutes more material than they are used to.

### *The five act structure*

John Yorke, BBC Controller of Drama Production & New Talent, teaches the five act structure for continuing drama (basically the second act of the three act structure is split into three). He identifies that one of the weaknesses of the three act structure in television drama is the long second act, which has the potential to lose focus. Robert McKee, in *Story: Substance, Structure, Style and the Principles of Screenwriting*, also notes that the weak point of a screenplay is invariably in the middle of the second act, where even a well-written story can get bogged down.

The five act structure is taken from Shakespeare, who in turn borrowed it from the ancient Romans, Horace and Terence.

In simple terms, the **five acts** are:

1. **Set up and inciting incident.**
   *(Macbeth hears the witches' prophesy and realises the throne could be his.)*

2. **Initial objectives achieved.**
   *(Macbeth kills Duncan and becomes King.)*

3. **Things start to go wrong.**
   *(Banquo is killed, but Fleance escapes. Macduff defects.)*

4. **Things get worse precipitating crisis.**
   *(Lady Macbeth kills herself. England resolves to attack.)*

5. **Matters resolved in final battle.**
   *(Macbeth defeated, order restored.)*

The length of each act varies according to the duration of the programme – in *Casualty* each of the five acts is approximately 10 minutes long; in *Doctors* approximately five minutes. At the end of each act, there should be a turning point, where 'the world changes' with a 'character changing moment'. This could be a quiet or explosive moment, but it presents 'some new obstacle' significantly altering the inner or external landscape for one character. Yorke highlights, however, the importance of making these character turning points plausible. (Applying the same principle of turning points, a 90-minute drama should have seven acts).

Taking his cue from successful American drama series like *ER*, he advises writing as if there are ad breaks. Before the first ad break, the protagonist is thrown into a different world. Before the fourth ad break, there's a big 'explosion', metaphorical or real. In an ensemble show with multiple storylines like *Casualty* or *ER*, Yorke explains that the protagonist is the staff – the characters 'hand the baton' from one to the other during the course of the episode. Thus, in an *ER* episode Doug Ross will wake up to start the day in Act One, but by Act Four Peter Benton will come in and have to perform an urgent operation.

Here is an illustration of the five acts in an episode of Casualty.

***Casualty: 'Farmead Menace: Part One' written by Mark Catley. Episode 1, Series 23, transmitted 13 September 2008.***

The main stories follow a television crew making a documentary about the A&E department amidst the spectacular and explosive repercussions of a teenage girl on a housing estate setting off a firework in a block of flats. As the first episode of the season, the episode serves the purpose of reintroducing the main characters, delineating continuing storylines and identifying the themes of the show for regular viewers and the potential new audience. '*Farmead Menace*' was a two-part story and the episode ended with a number of cliffhanger plots to be resolved in the next episode broadcast the following day.

*Casualty* follows different types of staff – nurses (Charlie, Tess, Jessica, Alice and Kelsey), doctors (Adam, Ruth, Toby and Zoe), paramedics (Dixie, Jeff, Curtis and Shczena) and the porter (Big Mac). '*Farmead Menace Part 1*' focuses on the characters Tess, Zoe, Adam, Dixie and Jeff.

**Act One** focuses on the staff of the A&E department being interviewed for a television documentary. This reveals the different personalities and professional commitment of the regular characters and their conflicting views on the role of healthcare and the community. The first act 'passes the baton' between a stressed Tess;

Adam talking about Jessica, who he had an affair with; Curtis and Alice making eyes at each other; and Zoe being removed from her job. There are also the first sights of a young cancer patient being treated in the A&E department; the teenage Sammy in a fight, running along the street and collecting fireworks; and the helpful Vic supporting some of the more vulnerable people of the community. The act concludes with Zoe being advised by a hospital manager to stop acting alone and learn to be part of the family: this is Zoe's own dramatic journey and reinforces the importance, within this episode and the show, of the staff working together.

**Act Two** commences with a humorous scene from one of the secondary characters, Big Mac, who talks about the need for the television crew to film those who don't usually have a voice, but when offered the opportunity to speak he can't think of anything to say (this becomes a storyline and theme in the second episode). On the Farmead Estate, Vic visits an old man and an elderly woman and grandson with learning difficulties; Sammy sets off a firework in the block of flats, resulting in injuries to herself, the old man and the elderly woman and setting off a metaphorical ticking bomb that will explode with devastating consequences later in the episode. The television crew follow the paramedics, Jeff and Dixie; Adam tries to find a way to influence Jessica to commit to their relationship; and Tess works at remaining calm. The act ends with Tess reporting 'nothing will bother (her) today' as she walks into a cubicle and finds an injured and aggressive Sammy.

**Act Three** starts with a humorous scene with the paramedics arriving at the block of flats, with the television crew, and being joined by Adam. It moves onto Kelsey and Zoe arguing over a young cancer patient; Tess in conflict with Sammy; and the medics treating the elderly woman. The tensions in the plots continue to build and at the midpoint of the episode (25 minutes), a devastating explosion occurs. The paramedics work to save the elderly woman amidst an inferno as Adam acts, in a running theme for the episode, as a 'superhero', in order to rescue the old man. The act ends with Tess in an argument with Charlie, her manager.

**Act Four** begins with Adam rescuing the old man and saying that he 'can't let paramedics have all the glory. I have an old flame to rekindle'. The next scene has his lover Jessica arriving at the hospital. The act moves between the paramedics trying to escape the block of flats; Zoe warming to the young cancer patient; Tess finding her office wrecked and a swastika daubed over the wall and leaving the hospital (reportedly to 'have a break' but unable to chill); Jeff and Adam making up, following disagreements they had rescuing the injured; and Jeff and Dixie trying to save the life of the elderly woman who has now stopped breathing. The act ends with Tess following her personal mission and going to Sammy's house, being intimidated by her family and getting out, without being assaulted.

**Act Five** resolves some of the individual stories, links two stories which had been separate and ratchets up the tension overall. The act begins with Adam returning to the hospital and making choices based on developing his relationship with Jessica; Jeff and Dixie saving the life of the elderly woman; Zoe comforting the young cancer patient; and Tess running after Sammy across a building site, falling, spearing herself and being unable to move. Sammy runs away and hides. As Jeff and Dixie are driving in the ambulance to the hospital and celebrating, in front of the television camera, saving the elderly woman, Sammy runs into the path of the ambulance. Shockingly the ambulance ploughs into her and she is thrown into the air. Dixie stares at the mangled body and Jeff shouts for her to get the medical equipment to save the girl. Meanwhile Tess is screaming in pain, injured and alone on the building site.

This episode has multiple storylines, act breaks every 10 minutes and an episode midpoint which significantly increases the sense of jeopardy for the main characters. It moves between the individual stories featuring the main characters and guest characters, 'passing on the baton', and is constructed effectively to deliver a balance of suspense, humour and character moments. The individual plots are character-driven: for instance only Tess would leave the hospital in the way she does, to pursue the troublesome patient. This episode also sets up future events in the storylines (of this two-parter and later episodes) through character actions and in dialogue exchanges, creating a sense of resonance for alert and regular viewers.

*Neil Penswick: extracted from 'Television Drama: The Five Act Structure', an essay for the De Montfort University MA TV Scriptwriting.*

John Yorke says that many writers fail on structure, which is why he places such emphasis on getting it right. He states that a five act structure 'gives you a shape' and that its use by dramatists over the centuries demonstrates that 'it works'. However, he stresses that what is important is 'great story not great structure'.

'For me, structure is the most difficult part of script-writing. I therefore spend what seems like a dispropor-tionate amount of time working on a treatment/storyline which is very long and very explicit. This is more than a "warm up" for the script, it's actually a kind of "dry run" in the sense that I try to nail the narrative

structure in such a document. At the same time, given that character journeys are often the spine or the "RSJ" of storytelling, I begin the process of "familiarity" with character. We won't be immediately acquainted until I write the script but at the same time, their presence in the treatment has to give a reader (and me) a full insight into who they are and where they're going. To get into them quite fully before the script I write dialogue scenes in the treatment to get the sound of their voice and WHAT they may say. Having ventured the relationship metaphor with scripts, I'd say that a treatment has to feel like much more than a first date, a first impression. For me, it's feeling like I've been "going out" with the treatment (structure and character) before I'm ready to "commit" to a script.'
*Tony Marchant* (Garrow's Law, Holding On, The Mark of Cain)

## Planning the script: creating a treatment

It is better to work out the structure of a script before you start writing, rather than making it up as you go along. This doesn't mean that it is not going to have to be endlessly rewritten – Matthew Graham's first episode of *Life on Mars* went through 35 drafts! – but a lot of time can be saved if the basic shape of the script is sound and you know where you are going when you start writing.

It is a good idea to write a **treatment**. It does not need to be more than five to seven pages, but it should have a clear dramatic structure and should contain all of the key events in the narrative. Many experienced writers dislike the idea of writing detailed treatments and would rather get on with the script after having an idea accepted. Nevertheless, before a writer is actually commissioned to write a first draft of the script, the television commissioning process often requires a treatment followed by a **scene-by-scene breakdown**. This contains the details of every scene in the story and is the equivalent of a step outline for a feature film.

From an initial outline of the story, you can begin to decide how many scenes there are going to be and what happens in each scene. It is very easy at this stage to change the order of scenes and to work out the most effective way of telling the story.

> Most TV drama series construct their episodes around the three storyline principle. There is usually an **A** story, in which there is most at stake, a slightly less important **B** story and a **C** story, which will have the least scenes and with the least at stake will often provide comic relief. This structure allows inter-cutting to shift both story and time forward. It helps develop characters through different storylines (work and domestic life) and takes pressure off the writer who has to fill 60 minutes of drama.

Some writers find it helpful to have an index card for each scene, so they can physically move the scenes around. This is particularly useful in the case of a television series episode when there are a number of story strands to weave together – a typical episode of *Casualty* will have six storylines: three for the regular characters and three for the guests. Each story strand can be allocated a different coloured card and the running order can be adjusted and refined before the first draft of the script is written. There is also software available that can do this. One of my ex-students, Harriet Smart, has designed Writer's Café (www.writerscafe.co.uk) where there are a number of useful tools for fiction writers.

## Synopsis, outline, treatment

A **synopsis** can be one long paragraph, or several paragraphs; probably no more than a page-and-a-half in length; normally less, usually focused on plot. It's often a concise distillation of a story that already exists in longer form, such as the synopsis of a script found in script coverage (a script report written by a script reader in a film or television company).

An **outline** or **story outline** is sometimes used interchangeably with a synopsis – but in fact they're almost always a bit longer, with more detail, more emphasis on character, tone, and theme, and are not solely plot-driven.

A **treatment** consists of a condensation of the proposed film or TV dramatic production, written in the present tense. It covers the basic ideas and issues of the production, as well as the main characters, locations, and story angles. It should be attention-getting and interesting to read – it should make the reader want to read the script – and should cover the full story sequence, with everything resolved.

The detail in the treatment is for the writer's benefit as well as for the reader, script editor and producer.

(There are examples of a synopsis, an outline and a treatment in the Appendix at the end of this book. These are for an episode of Jim Hill's *Otters Reach*, a drama series commissioned but not produced by the BBC.)

## Tell, don't show: writing a treatment

Jim Hill, co-creator of *Boon*, sets out the following elements of a good treatment.

### *Treatment of the plot*

- Told chronologically.
- Told in present tense.
- Reveals external *and* internal conflict.
- Shows action: describes how the script develops the plot and characterisation.
- Provides the resolution: how loose ends are tied up, plot points or beats, revelations, surprise endings.
- Reveals subplots.

### *Treatment of major characters*

- Describes their careers.
- Highlights their relevant background: adds to conflict, characterisation or resolution.
- Shows internal conflicts.
- Explains the motivation of major characters.

### *Treatment of the setting*

- Sets the time period of story.
- Establishes the amount of time that lapses.
- Pinpoints geographic locations.

*Never* include . . .

- A physical description of characters unless the information is *critical* to the plot or the characterisation.

- Details of secondary, minor or background (stock) characters unless *critical* to conflict or plot resolution.
- Dialogue unless the plot can't be explained without it.
- Any 'editorial' comment that attempts to directly persuade the reader as to what a good story it is.

**Remember: if the treatment is boring, the script won't be read.**

## Scene by scene

Once you have written your treatment you will have a detailed short story (without dialogue). Your next objective is to turn this into a scene by scene document. The point of the scene by scene is to create as many scenes, from the treatment, as possible to help you write the script and to help you write the dialogue.

Jim Hill explains that a scene by scene is what it says – a scene-by-scene expansion of your treatment. It is not the treatment simply divided up into scene headings. You will need to 'expand on' and 'extract from' the treatment to see how many scenes you may (or can) have. In the process you will have to clarify your scenes and determine what they are about.

A **scene** is:

- a dramatic unit
- a stand alone unit
- the framework for dramatic interaction between characters – often involving conflict.

A **scene by scene breakdown**:

- is a road map to the script. It offers directions, lets the writer feel confident they can rearrange material and most of all is a guide to the dialogue content of each scene

- offers a guide to a draft script structure – making script changes less stressful. Are your scenes in the right order? Is there a structure problem? Does a scene give away information too soon – or too late? Do scenes need to be swapped around? *It is easier to rearrange a scene by scene of 70 or so scenes than to unpick a draft of a script.*

Jim demonstrates how breaking your script into bite-size scenes allows you to see:

- do you have enough material?
- are you clear on what each scene is meant to deliver?
- what will be the dialogue content of each scene?

### Do you have enough material?

Working on a scene by scene will soon show you whether you have enough story, i.e. whether you will be able to deliver a first draft script of the required length. You may discover that your initial idea is going to require further development, additional twists and turns or subplots, before you can start writing the script. However, it can be difficult to judge the length of a script, particularly for an inexperienced writer. Aiming for a specific number of pages is not always easy or helpful; thinking in terms of scenes required is a better approach. A one-hour script will be between 70 and 90 scenes. If given a page count, writers often struggle to fit their script in. Given a target of 70–90 scenes, a writer can feel there is some flexibility.

### Are you clear on what each scene is meant to deliver?

Scenes contain location, action, description, characters and dialogue. Importantly they contain the motivation and agenda of *your* characters. When breaking a treatment into scenes, clarify the mood, agenda and motivation of the character(s) within it.

---

### Sample

The opening paragraph from the *Otters Reach* treatment (see Appendix, page 251).

A battered car pulls to a halt in a country lane. The driver, KELLOWAY goes to the boot of the car and opens it. He lifts out an injured and bleeding dog and dumps it in the ditch at the side of the road. KELLOWAY drives off. The abandoned dog struggles to get up but cannot.

How many scenes is this?

1) EXT COUNTRY LANE DAY 1
A battered car pulls to a halt. The driver, KELLOWAY, feral youth, goes to the boot of the car and opens it. He lifts out an injured and bleeding dog and dumps it in the ditch at the side of the road. KELLOWAY drives off. The abandoned dog struggles to get up but cannot.

Here it is one scene all filmed by a static camera, all the action is seen in a single frame.

OR

It could be 5 scenes with detail about KELLOWAY – his reactions to the dog, his attitude. Is he playing music, laughing, annoyed or upset?

1 EXT COUNTRY ROAD DAY 1
The establishing shot of the road. (Music over?)

---

2 INT CAR DAY 1
KELLOWAY, a feral youth, drives. He **reacts** to the sound of a whimpering dog. KELLOWAY pulls up and gets out.

3) EXT COUNTRY ROAD DAY 1
KELLOWAY goes to the boot, lifts and dumps dog and gets into car.

4) INT CAR DAY 1
KELLOWAY drives off – is he **relieved or guilty?** Give him a reaction.

5) EXT DITCH DAY 1
Shot of the dog in the ditch.

*(© Jim Hill)*

### *What will be the dialogue content of each scene?*

All characters have motivation and agendas. What is your character's overall motivation and agenda for your story? What is their motivation and agenda in each scene?

- What are they feeling? What is their emotional level?
- What's the subtext? What are they not saying?

This is your drama. You know the characters. You have plotted this out. What are they feeling, thinking, or planning? Your scene by scene should help clarify the relationships and agendas of all the characters in a scene. What don't they know?

This detail goes a long way to helping you write dialogue.

## Sample

ALICE & BOB come out of their apartment, cross the lobby and enter the lift. In the lift they discuss their planned visit to ALICE'S mother, ROSE.

As two simple scenes:

1 INT LOBBY DAY
ALICE & BOB come out of their apartment, cross the lobby and enter the lift.

2 INT LIFT DAY
In the lift they discuss their planned visit to ALICE'S mother, ROSE.

If these were your characters, what would you know about them?

- Are they in agreement?
- Do they disagree?
- What is ALICE'S relationship with her mother?
- What is BOB'S?
- Is there a **subtext** – perhaps BOB is not responding to ALICE'S questions or comments?

By considering these questions the scene can now look like this:

2 INT LIFT DAY
In the lift ALICE raises the subject of their planned visit to ALICE'S mother, ROSE. BOB reminds ALICE that she planned the visit, not him.

How does that play as dialogue?

(There is friction now, which introduces dramatic conflict.)

(© Jim Hill)

**Sample**

JOHN & JACK are business partners but have financial problems. JOHN visits JACK. JOHN greets JACK. They talk about their money issues. JOHN is determined on settling the debt while JACK isn't. JACK eventually responds to JOHN'S suggestions.

This lacks definition – of character, mood and agendas.

Choose any of the following words in bold to give the eventual dialogue some energy.

JOHN greets JACK **enthusiastically/aggressively/ dismissively**.
They then **chat/argue/discuss** their money issues.
JOHN is **forceful/demanding/resigned** about settling the debt while JACK remains **vague/dismissive/unconcerned**. JACK eventually responds to JOHN'S suggestions to settle the debt **positively/unenthusiastically/reluctantly**.

**DEFINITION & CLARIFICATION = DIALOGUE**

*(© Jim Hill)*

If you have gone through the process of writing a treatment and a scene by scene breakdown first, you will be in a much stronger position when you start writing the script. You will have the confidence of knowing that the story works, that the structure is sound and that you have enough material. You will also find it easier to write the dialogue if you have already considered the characters' agendas in each scene.

# 12 Hooking an audience

## The first 10 pages

The BBC writersroom (www.bbc.co.uk/writersroom) will only give an unsolicited script a full read if it makes it past the ten-page sift stage. Every script is given 10 pages to hook the reader and, if it doesn't, it will be rejected. This may seem harsh, but this is a direct reflection of the way the television audience responds. If you don't hook that audience in the first few minutes, they will change channels and they won't come back.

This doesn't mean that you always have to begin with explosions and smoking tyres, but it does mean that you have to hit the ground running. In the cinema the audience is more committed. Its members, having made a decision to be there, bought their tickets and settled into their seats, are unlikely to walk out if the first 10 minutes seem a little slow. Thus, the script can afford to take its time setting the scene. However, a television audience is not a captive or tolerant audience and time is not on the side of the writer. The emotional engagement of the audience is the ultimate goal of any script and this needs to be achieved as quickly as possible.

The first 10 pages need to establish:

- the main characters
- the genre
- the tone

- what the story is about
- what is at stake.

## The main characters

*Empathy*

Robert McKee, in *Story*, states that it is 'the glue of empathy' that holds the audience's emotional involvement. This glue is vital if the audience is going to care about your characters and what happens to them. This is what Aristotle meant when he said that pity, along with fear and catharsis, are essential ingredients for successful drama.

From the beginning, common ground needs to be established with the reader/audience. Christopher Vogler says that this is the function of the first stage, the ordinary world, of the archetypal hero's journey. We need to know what makes the characters tick and what motivates them, so that we can see the world from their point of view. We may not necessarily sympathise with them, they may even be objectionable, but we need to understand them. In my experience, most scripts that fail fail because the motivation of the characters is not consistent or credible and any hope of empathy in the reader is lost.

The more screen time an audience actually spends with a character, the more they are prepared to go along with them. When he adapted *Pride and Prejudice*, Andrew Davies wanted to redress the balance of the novel, as he disclosed in *The Daily Telegraph* (18 February 2011):

> 'Jane Austen wrote *Pride and Prejudice* from Elizabeth's point of view. But the story is just as much Darcy's. So I allow the audience to see Darcy on his own, or with other men, enabling us to know him better, and like him more.'

We spend so much time with Dexter Morgan in *Dexter* or with Tony Soprano and his 'family' in *The Sopranos* that we inevitably tend to side with them, even if we don't necessarily approve of their actions or subscribe to their moral code.

'In the past I've written about Motor Neurone Disease *(Goodbye Cruel World)*, Credit Unions *(Never Never)* and New Towns *(Take Me Home)*. They don't seem like promising or enticing subjects for drama but I'd like to think I succeeded in locating WHERE the drama was for an audience. And that's the theme behind the subjects in those shows — grief, greed and debt, the yearning for freedom. However ostensibly "dry" a subject appears, as long as you also locate what is most visceral and emotional, as long as you find the universal conflicts that an audience can recognise, you're nearly there. I say nearly because ultimately you can't deliver high emotion without compelling storytelling. Therefore, in *Never Never*, John Simm was a loan shark but also the most charismatic shit you're ever likely to meet. In *Goodbye Cruel World*, Sue Johnston was left to die, her body closing down bit by bit, while Alun Armstrong, her husband, built a successful charity on her behalf because he was an emotional coward who loved her but couldn't face her death and sought refuge in fundraising. I've made a career out of making tough subjects watchable by trying to pay attention to the absolute need to connect.'

*Tony Marchant*

*Introducing characters*

How characters are introduced can reveal a lot about them and should be carefully considered. We need to see them in their world and how they operate within it before the main story gets underway. If the audience does not engage with them at this point, they will not go with them on their journey.

It is always advisable to reveal character through action. Sam Tyler in *Life on Mars* (Matthew Graham) chases, arrests and then questions a murder suspect. Giacomo Casanova in *Casanova* (Russell T Davies), escaping from a lover's husband, is chased through the streets of Venice. Fitz in *Cracker* (Jimmy McGovern) listens to the closing stages of a horserace on a payphone before delivering a bizarre guest lecture to university students, subverting their and our expectations by throwing books at his audience. Jonathan Creek in *Jonathan Creek* (David Renwick), in a supermarket queue, rightly suspects that the till is faulty and is overcharging the customers, but he receives little gratitude from his fellow shoppers, who are delayed while this is checked out. In each case, we are not told what these characters are like, but the action they are involved in lets us see this for ourselves.

The *Jonathan Creek* scene is an interesting example. It has little to do with the story of the episode, but David Renwick has found a very entertaining way of introducing his central character. We meet Jonathan in a normal everyday situation, but from the reactions of those around him can see that he doesn't really fit in. His brilliant mind is exhibited, but his shaggy appearance and the contents of his shopping basket – two cheese sandwiches and a Barbie doll – mark him down as some kind of 'weirdo'. The next scene in his windmill home shows him sawing off the head of the Barbie doll as he devises another stage trick for magician, Adam Klaus, but the scene in the supermarket illustrates that we can learn as much from the reactions of others to them, as we can from characters' own actions.

Fitz in *Cracker* is a brilliant criminal psychologist. However, he is a flawed character; his private life is a mess. He is unfaithful to his wife, he drinks too much, he smokes too much and he gambles too much. It is these character weaknesses that make him human and give the audience, who may find his 'world' alien to them, something to identify with – they find common ground.

Detective Chief Inspector Jane Tennison in *Prime Suspect* is a tough, successful woman in a wholly male environment. However, the pressure of her job takes its toll on her private life and her ability to sustain a long-term meaningful relationship. Brittle at the best of times, she eventually becomes an alcoholic. In spite of her success, Jane Tennison is always vulnerable.

Characters with no apparent vulnerabilities are difficult for audiences to relate to and, most importantly, to care about. Fitz and Jane Tennison are prime examples of the kind of complex, well-rounded, engaging central characters that successful television drama series need.

In *Only Fools and Horses* John Sullivan wanted to base a show on the character, the fly pitcher, he and producer, Ray Butt, remembered with affection from their time working in London street-markets. Worried that the audience might not warm to a dodgy guy, who is a bit of a 'toe-rag', he gave him a kid brother, 14 years younger, that he had brought up since their mother had died. Thus, Del Boy and Rodney were created. Not only does this make Del Boy a more sympathetic character, it is the warmth of his relationship with Rodney that is at the heart of the show. It is what the audience relates to and what keeps on bringing them back.

## The genre and tone

Is it a drama, a comedy or a thriller? More specifically – is it a crime drama, a romantic comedy or a fantasy? The longer it takes a reader to work out exactly what they are reading, the longer they will spend detached from the script and neither engaged with the characters nor absorbed by the story.

If it is not immediately clear what type of story is being told (the genre) and how seriously it should be taken (the tone), the audience will not be comfortable. In simple terms the viewer needs to know if it is their kind of thing. The decisions we make about what to watch, on television as well as at the cinema, are invariably linked to genre. Movie posters, trailers, on-screen promotions make the genre very clear in order to attract an audience. The casual viewer will look elsewhere if they don't feel their expectations are going to be satisfied.

The tone is clearly set in the very first moment of *Casanova* (see page 218). Casanova, caught in the act by an irate husband, escapes onto the balcony and whistles up his white charger. The horse gallops towards him, Casanova jumps ... and misses. The horse gallops past and Casanova lands on the ground. The first line of dialogue is 'Bollocks.' Although this is a BBC period drama, we are clearly not in the world of Jane Austen or the ladies of Cranford!

The first 10 pages of the first episode of *Life on Mars* introduce Sam Tyler and show how his personal life and his professional life as a police officer are closely interlinked. A murder investigation is already underway and when his colleague and girlfriend, Maya, is apparently abducted by the killer, Sam's distress is plain to see. His mind elsewhere he is hit by a car and wakes up in 1973. At the bottom of page 10 he asks a confused copper 'What's going on?' This is exactly what the reader and the audience want to know too. By this point it is clear what the story is about and what is at stake. The past is a foreign country, or in this case another planet, and we are firmly 'with' Sam as he begins to explore this alien environment. After the serious crime drama of the opening sequence, a more light-hearted tone is established in the conversation, full of misunderstandings, with the copper:

SAM

. . . I need my mobile.

COPPER

Your mobile what?

One decision that has to be made with any story is where to begin to tell it. How much information, how much back story, does the audience need to know? It is often the case that the first scene of a script can be cut because there is nothing in it that is not established elsewhere. On more than one occasion when an episode of *The Upper Hand* was over-running, we realised we could lose the first scene without losing any of the story. In the shooting script of *Life on Mars* (available at www.bbc.co.uk/writersroom) the first two scenes are set in Sam's loft apartment with its widescreen plasma television and other hi-tech appliances. This sequence establishes that Sam's relationship with Maya is going through a bad patch and also what Sam's lifestyle is like 'now' (before he goes back into the past). Matthew Graham realised that a later exchange in the police station establishes the former and that the latter is redundant as the contemporary television audience does not need to be shown what life is like 'now'. Without these scenes, the finished episode opens with a shot of speeding police cars, swiftly followed by a chase and a suspect taken into custody. An arresting opening for a television drama!

## What the story is about and what is at stake

It is the **inciting incident** (something happens, which throws the main character's life out of balance), which introduces conflict, gets the story rolling and hooks the audience's interest. Anything before this is simply set-up. Once the audience know where they are (the world of the story) and who they are watching (the characters), this should happen as soon as possible. However, there are no hard and fast rules – some stories need more set-up than others.

In an episode of a continuing series (drama or comedy), where the audience is familiar with the territory, the story can get underway in the first scene. This can even happen in a first episode. The inciting incident is in the first scene of *Dawson's Creek*. Dawson and Joey, both 15, are lying together on Dawson's bed. Joey tells Dawson that she no longer feels it is appropriate that she should 'sleep over' with him and share his bed. Their 'emerging hormones' are destined to alter their relationship. Dawson disagrees, saying 'It doesn't apply to us ... We can still remain friends, despite any mounting sexual theoretics.' This conversation sets them both on a new journey. We already know what the story is about: *Dawson's Creek* is a teenage *When Harry Met Sally*, which endeavours to answer the question 'Can a man and a woman just be friends?'

The story is always about what the characters want and what might prevent them from getting it. This needs to be clearly established early in your script. If it is not clear what obstacles need to be overcome, then the goal will seem easily achievable and the audience, anticipating an uneventful story, will not stay with it. The more that is at stake the better – the more powerful the forces of antagonism, the stronger the story.

The audience needs to have enough information to be in a position to weigh up the odds and to anticipate what is and is not likely to happen. The main tension of any drama is the balance between *hope* and *fear*. We hope the main character will achieve their goal, but we fear they may not. We hope for the best, but fear the worst. Unexpected twists and turns in the plot will keep the audience's pulses racing, but it is the ups and downs as the balance shifts between hope and fear that will keep the audience emotionally involved in your story and keen to know what happens next.

# 13 Holding an audience

## Moving the story forward

When I first started working as a script editor at ATV, Shaun O'Riordan, who had just finished producing the cult sci-fi series *Sapphire & Steel*, handed me a script and told me to go through it, noting down the plot function of each scene. Not what happened in each scene – a synopsis – but *what each scene did*. This is an extremely useful exercise for a writer, because it enables you objectively to determine how important or relevant each scene is, regardless of its content. If the scene does not have a plot function – if it is not moving the story forward or is not revealing something about character – then it shouldn't be there. There is one exception to this rule – if it is funny. Humour is of course very appealing, but if a script is over-running, it will be hard to justify a funny scene if it isn't contributing something vital to the story.

## Coming in late and getting out early

Inexperienced writers tend to over-write – scenes will be too long, characters will talk too much. If you are clear what the function of a scene is, then it is easier to trim it to its essential elements. In other words, come into the scene just before the crucial moment, get to the point and once you've made it, get out quickly. Unnecessary preambles and extended action will get in the way and will slow the script down. Don't waste screen time. In less hurried times, television dramas showed characters arriving and leaving – lots of shots of cars driving up and people entering buildings – but the modern audience is accustomed to more pace and doesn't need everything to be spelled out.

## Make 'em laugh, make 'em cry . . . make 'em wait

Who shot JR? *(Dallas)*. Who killed Laura Palmer? *(Twin Peaks)*. Who shot Phil Mitchell? *(EastEnders)*. Why did Mary Alice kill herself? *(Desperate Housewives)*. From *Dallas* and *Twin Peaks* to Albert Square and Wisteria Lane, television has always hooked huge audiences and built them by delaying gratification as long as possible. Good storytelling keeps the audience guessing, not only over the course of a series or between series, but also scene by scene. There were numerous occasions in *Dallas* when JR or Bobby would phone one another to announce they had important news. However, in spite of the urgency of the situation they never seemed to have time to give any details and would always tell the other to meet them later at Southfork!

Jurgen Wolff, screenwriter and writing coach, recommends considering what questions each scene can raise in the audience. Subsequent scenes should pose new questions, while answering some of the questions that have gone before. He points out, though, that questions are easy and answers are not. In his opinion *Lost* 'failed', because it kept on raising questions and not answering them. If a scene raises a question and then answers it straightaway, it is a wasted opportunity. Withholding information will keep the audience watching and increase the dramatic tension.

In the first scene of *Downton Abbey*, a telegram arrives down the wire in the village post office. The postmistress reads it.

> POSTMISTRESS
>
> Oh my god.

The Postmaster comes over to look at it:

> POSTMASTER
>
> That's impossible. I'll take it up there now.
>
> POSTMISTRESS
>
> Don't be stupid. None of them will be up for hours. What difference will it make? Jimmy will do it when he comes in.

A bad scene would have revealed the contents of the message. This scene creates interest and concern. It is several scenes later before the telegram is handed to Robert Crawley, Earl of Grantham, at breakfast. Ashen-faced he leaves the room without comment after reading it. In the next scene, the final scene of part one, we finally discover that James and Patrick have perished on the *Titanic*. However, we do not know who they are and the real significance of the news – that the heir to Robert Crawley's title and estate is dead – is still held back from us.

## Cliffhangers

Who shot JR? was the most famous cliffhanger in TV history. JR Ewing was shot in the final scene of the 1979–80 season of *Dallas* and the US audience, and the rest of the world, had to wait from March until November 1980 to find out who did it. The culprit was revealed to be Kristin Shepard, JR's scheming sister-in-law and mistress, but most of the rest of the cast of course had been prime suspects. 76% of all television viewers in the USA watched the first episode of the 1980–81 season and 'the television industry learned the power of the cliffhanger season finale'. (*New York Times*, 7 May 1995). Fifteen years later even *The Simpsons* got in on the act with their final season episode 'Who Shot Mr Burns?'. Suspects naturally included Homer, Bart, Lisa, Principal Skinner, Grampa Simpson, Smithers and Tito Puente!

Cliffhangers were employed in nineteenth century serialised novels and in popular silent film series and today feature regularly in television series, particularly soaps. In fact to most people the drum beats from *EastEnders'* closing music are synonymous with the very idea of a television cliffhanger ending. Although cliffhangers are generally at the end of an episode or before a commercial break, to bring the audience back, there is no reason why every scene shouldn't end this way. Thinking in terms of cliffhangers will give your storytelling a strong narrative drive and will keep the audience wanting to know what will happen next. The secret is to cut away to the next scene as soon as something dramatic or unexpected is revealed to the audience.

A cliffhanger is invariably a turning point, which subverts the protagonist's and, crucially, the audience's expectations. In our house a season of *24* has always been rated on the number of times my wife exclaimed 'Oh my god!' at crucial plot twists. On this basis the show dipped after the first couple of seasons, but improved considerably later on! The more OMG moments you can work into your script, the more attractive it will be to the audience. However, it is important to remember that such moments only really work and are only truly satisfying if they are entirely credible. If they feel contrived and are not properly set up, then you will lose your audience.

E.M. Forster said, 'Surprise me with the believable'. The best writing takes the audience by surprise, but also takes the audience with it.

> 'A plausible impossibility is preferable to an implausible possibility.'
> *Aristotle*

## Turning points

Robert McKee says that 'each turning point hooks curiosity'. The audience wonders what will happen next, as the protagonist is put at increasingly greater risk. Turning points spin the story round and propel it forward in another direction. Without them scripts are boring and predictable and lacking in drama. Characters go on journeys and those journeys require turning points. The longer the journey the more turning points there will be. A sitcom story may only need one turning point, but a one-hour drama or a feature film will require more.

In the second season *Frasier* episode 'You Scratch My Book', Frasier is smitten by Dr Honey Snow, a voluptuous author of very soppy, inspirational self-help books. Although he is scathing about her behind her back, calling her books 'absolute drivel', he is delighted when she invites him to join her for dinner. However, the turning point in the story comes when Honey hands him the manuscript of her forthcoming book and invites Frasier to write the foreword. Frasier has no choice, but to agree. (End of Part One.)

Each story strand in a script should have its own turning point(s). In the same *Frasier* episode Niles invests $500 of Daphne's money with his new stockbroker. The $500 grows to $700 and Niles is thrilled when Daphne rewards him with a kiss and a hug. He persuades her to let him re-invest her profits and gets more kisses from Daphne as the stock rises. The turning point comes when Frasier catches Niles out – Niles has been pretending the stock has been rising, even though he has lost Daphne's money. Niles is forced to change tack.

Characters will be forced by circumstance to take actions they have previously condemned or not had the courage or desire to attempt. The choices they make will create turning points and these moments must be dramatised for the audience – they must be shown. Not only are such moments the very stuff of drama, but denied seeing them the audience may have difficulty accepting or believing them. We need to know and to understand why characters have to change. If it is not clear how a character arrives at a particular point on their journey or reaches a particular decision, then the script isn't working.

## Character building

Rather than building up full character biographies (like where they went to school), writer Tony Jordan (*EastEnders, Life on Mars, Hustle*) focuses on three things: something they would always do, something they would never do and a paradox. The paradox may be in the character's situation – a man who wants the finest things in life works in a run-down, second-class hotel (Basil Fawlty) – but it is also in their personality. This paradox is important because it is the difference between two-dimensional characters and three-dimensional characters. It is what gives your characters depth and makes them more interesting and engaging.

The best characters have contradictory elements within them and often it is the resolution of these internal conflicts that enables them to change, which is what drama is all about. (It is when characters can't or won't change that tragedy ensues.) A character may be ambitious, but scared of success; altruistic, but selfish; looking for love, but afraid of commitment. The best stories are character driven and it is these contradictions that can lead to situations and to stories.

Hamlet, one of the most fascinating and complex characters in dramatic literature, is a mass of contradictions. He wants to avenge his father, yet he is reluctant to kill his uncle. When faced with a choice, he can't decide what to do, 'To be, or not to be: that is the question'. Characters in drama are forced to make choices – whether in *Frasier*, *Hamlet* or *EastEnders* – but the audience is put into the position of making the choices as well and wanting to tell the characters what to do. In *Developing Characters for Script Writing*, Rib Davis points out that:

> 'making choices on behalf of characters is very involving, pulling the audience closer and closer into the action, which is precisely what needs to happen if a script is to be successful'.

Characters without contradictions, however minor, are in danger of becoming stereotypes rather than individuals. If you ask a range of different people to describe somebody they all know, they will each come up with something slightly different. Of course most of what they say will be similar, but there will be subtle variations, some of them contradictory. Different people see different sides of us and we behave differently, according to who we are with and where we are. This is why hierarchies or pecking orders are so useful in comedy – Blackadder is obsequious to the Queen, but a bully to Baldrick – enabling the audience to enjoy seeing more than one side of a character.

Some writers, like Russell T Davies, seem to have the knack of coming up with characters and knowing who they are immediately – he even knows what their names are! Others prefer to build them up gradually by asking different questions about them and their background. Rib Davis recommends going through this process at the beginning because it can pay rich dividends later. He says that the ingredients that go into a character can be grouped into three categories (though they have huge areas of overlap).

- **What the character is born as/into** (nature/what we inherit e.g. gender, race, class, family background etc.).
- **What the character acquires or becomes through experience** (nurture e.g. education, abilities, sexuality etc.).
- **What the character is now** (this is what is most visible to the audience e.g. age, occupation, appearance, beliefs etc.).

Earlier in this book (see page 15), Julian expressed the view that a study of psychology was very valuable for any writer of fiction. Using the 'big five' personality traits developed by psychologists as a basis for your checklist, is another way of following Rib's advice. The big five are:

- **openness** (sometimes called intellect): imaginative and adventurous as opposed to conventional and cautious
- **conscientiousness:** self-disciplined and prepared as opposed to easy-going and careless
- **extraversion:** outgoing and energetic as opposed to introverted and reserved
- **agreeableness:** compassionate and co-operative as opposed to suspicious and cold
- **neuroticism** (sometimes called emotional stability): sensitive and nervous as opposed to relaxed and confident.

Tony Jordan applies for jobs in his character's name, using the questions on the application form as his checklist to help him understand the character. He even sends them off sometimes, claiming to have once got Gene Hunt (the Detective Chief Inspector from *Life on Mars*) a job as a night watchman!

### *Back-story*

It is not necessary for the audience to know as much about your characters as you do, but if you have taken the time to work out a detailed back-story and biography for them, you will have useful material to draw on as your series develops. The more you know about your characters, the more you will be able to make their actions consistent and credible. The audience will enjoy discovering more about them, as more information is revealed. One of the biggest moments in *EastEnders* was when Kat was forced to confront the incest she'd been subjected to and much about her character and previous behaviour finally became clear to the audience.

Barbara Machin, creator of *Waking the Dead*, advises paying particular attention to back-story when creating characters for a series:

'It took nine years in *Waking the Dead* before Boyd totally dealt with his personal cold case, his lost teenage son. All through that period it meant that he had a personal connection with each family story and parental anguish within the series. And he had to deal with the reality of living with an unsolved crime in his own life which gave him a particular take on every case both as a detective and as a member of the public. It allowed his team to orbit around his tragedy and it fuelled complex character engagement over these themes. Judicious embedding of back-story, designed to be excavated and explored, provides rich material and checks the very real genre danger of stories becoming too plot driven.'

Resonance for the characters will make your stories more interesting and more emotionally involving for the audience.

Rib Davis points out that the more of a character's background we are shown, the more we will understand the actions of the character, and the more sympathetic we are likely to be. This is comparable to a jury being presented with 'mitigating circumstances' by a barrister.

### *Pulling the strings*

The original poster for *My Fair Lady* on Broadway and in London showed a god-like George Bernard Shaw as a puppet-master on a cloud operating Rex Harrison's Henry Higgins and Julie Andrews' Eliza Doolittle as marionettes on the stage below him. When the audience is aware of the writer pulling the strings, they cease to engage with and believe in the characters. Shaun O'Riordan, back in my ATV days, used to talk about 'seeing the writer at work', when characters in a script behaved in a way that seemed unmotivated or inconsistent in order to service the plot.

Jimmy McGovern stresses that a writer should always be true to the characters. His first feature length drama for the BBC, *Needle*, was about Danny, a young heroin addict. In the story he had persistently lied to his wife, Paula, and she had thrown him out. McGovern wrote a scene, in which Danny sees Paula in the street with their child and pleads with her to stop and talk to him and eventually she does so. However, McGovern realised that whatever Danny said to Paula, she would have heard it all before and in reality would not have been persuaded by him and would have walked on by. As a writer he had a problem. He needed Paula to stop, but had to find a convincing reason for her to do so, no words he could put in Danny's mouth could be enough, however beautifully he crafted them. He was not being fair to Paula. In the end he had Danny running after Paula and, his attention diverted, colliding with an unseen lamp-post (a shock for him and the audience). Danny lies bleeding on the ground and Paula, in spite of herself, stops to see if he is all right. The solution to the problem was a dramatic shock, almost slapstick (McGovern says Charlie Chaplin has often come to his rescue!), but was totally convincing in terms of the characters.

### Every character has their reasons

The motivation of the antagonist should be just as clear to the audience as that of the protagonist. The best writing features antagonists that are as compelling as the protagonists and are not simply 'villains', there to serve the plot.

Jimmy McGovern is particularly adept at being able to see the world from the perspective of his antagonists, even when he disagrees with their point of view, and giving them a powerful voice. In 'Frankie's Story', the second episode of *Accused*, the sadistic bully, Corporal Buckley presents very persuasive arguments to justify his actions. This produces much more challenging drama for the audience.

### Who's who

It is important that characters are distinctive, but it is also important that characters are different from one another. It is these differences and the contrasts between the characters that create friction, create conflict and create drama. In comedy, this friction and conflict provides the humour. No matter how much they may have in common, in terms of background or status, each character needs to be an individual. The six characters in *Friends* are all very different, even though they are all of an age and are all 'friends'. They will each react differently to the same situation. They are not interchangeable. We can see this in the opening scenes of the very first episode. Ross is in the depths of depression over the ending of his marriage to Carol, who has come out as a lesbian, Joey sees this new bachelor status as something to be welcomed ('Strip joint!'), while Chandler reveals more of himself than he intended:

CHANDLER

Sometimes I wish I was a lesbian. (PAUSE) Did I say that out loud?

When building stories for your characters, Laurence Marks advises against referring to them as 'they'. Don't start off with a premise like 'they decide to go the cinema' or 'they resolve to take steps to deal with their financial problems'. Treat them as individuals. One character may want to go to the cinema; another may prefer to stay at home or may want to go to the gym. One character may want to make economies; another may prefer to bury their head in the sand and hope for the best. It is out of these situations that stories will evolve driven by the actions and reactions of the characters.

Making your characters distinctive also helps the reader and makes the script easier to read. Ben Stephenson (BBC Controller, Drama Commissioning) says he looks for empathetic, 'imitatable' characters. Often on the page a group of characters can merge together, which will lead to confusion as to who is who. There used to be something known as 'American casting'. In order to make it easier for audiences, if one female character was blonde then another was always dark or a brunette. If one male lead was tall and thin, another would be shorter and stockier etc. This of course is the same thinking behind the putting together of a boy band – the cute one, the sexy one, the moody one, the joker – or behind the assembling of the contestants for the *Big Brother* house. There is also the intention in these instances of having something for everyone and maximising the appeal of your 'product', but it is also about acknowledging the audience and keeping them involved.

There is always a danger that going too far down this route will lead to something formulaic, with a cast of characters that are each clearly filling a recognised stock role. The promising BBC1 drama series, *The Innocence Project*, about law students doing pro bono work to overturn miscarriages of justice, did not connect with an audience and was pulled from the schedules before it ended its run. *The Observer*'s television critic, Kathryn Flett, describing the series as 'blandly forgettable', referred to its cast of 'smug young law students' as 'cool cute guy', 'prissy uptight girl', 'nerd', 'feisty northern bird', 'babe' and 'bloke'. Just as the audience should not be aware of the writer at work, it is not going to be engaged by characters it senses have been lifted off the shelf marked pick 'n' mix.

## Dialogue

### *Show, don't tell*

Before you embark on your script, remember that television is a visual medium and that you are communicating with your audience through pictures. Always be aware of what the audience is looking at on the screen and consider how you can convey information without always relying on the dialogue. Andrew Davies never uses a line of dialogue if he can achieve the effect with a look. Writing in *The Daily Telegraph* (18 February 2011), he says:

> 'The most moving scene for me in *Pride and Prejudice* is the Pemberley music room scene: Elizabeth has just saved Darcy's sister from embarrassment, and as the music plays on, Darcy's look of gratitude becomes a look of love, which we see reciprocated in Elizabeth's eyes.'

Remember, it is *show* business, not *tell* business! If the audience is shown something, rather than told about it, it will have more impact. Equally, wherever possible, avoid characters recounting off-screen events. Show them to the audience. Reported action is boring compared to live action.

> 'If you can turn on the television, listen from another room and know everything that's happening, that's not television, it's radio.'
> *Linda Ellerbee*

The opening of the Channel 4 film *Yasmin* is a good example of visual storytelling. We see shots of a northern town, Keighley, as members of the Muslim community start their day: a man opens up his shop and cleans racist graffiti off the shutter, a young man calls the faithful to prayer. Behind a wall in a field outside the town a young Muslim woman, Yasmin, wriggles into a pair of jeans and removes her hijab. She approaches a convertible Golf GTI and enjoys zapping the remote central locking with her key fob, before getting in, putting on her sunglasses and driving off across the moors to work. Before there has been any dialogue we have been introduced to a spirited young woman, who is clearly living two lives in two different worlds. We have been *shown* the kind of woman Yasmin is and the dilemma she faces, even though we have not been *told* anything.

## *Less is more*

Don't make the dialogue do too much work. Long speeches should be avoided and any dialogue should be to the point. Inexperienced writers have a tendency to over-write and, just as individual scenes can be too long, so too can individual lines of dialogue. As Ray Frensham says in *Teach yourself: screenwriting*, 'Dialogue works best when it is underwritten and understated.' In a BBC4 *Screenwipe* interview, Tony Jordan recommends writers to keep taking words away, while making sure that the dialogue still makes sense:

> 'You may start with two guys coming out of a pub and they're going in opposite directions. One says:
>
> > *Great having a drink with you. Really enjoyed it. Great game of darts. I'm going home, going to have a shower and I'll see you later.*
>
> Keep taking words away and what you end up with is:
>
> > *Later.'*

This is actually how people talk and is all that this scene needs.

Unlike most actors, who will go through a script counting their lines, Michael Kitchen (Foyle in *Foyle's War*) famously keeps removing lines of dialogue, preferring to 'act' the emotions contained within them. We learn more about characters from what they do than from what they say. Remember to tell your story through your characters' actions.

Bad dialogue simply explains the plot to an audience. Rib Davis, author of *Writing Dialogue for Scripts*, believes that good dialogue should leave gaps for the audience to fill. The audience will pick up on hints or nuances and will draw their own conclusions. They don't need to be 'told' everything. Rib demonstrates that an active audience – an audience that has to do some work – is an involved audience. A passive audience, an audience that doesn't have to think, an audience that is spoon-fed information, is ultimately not a satisfied audience. As Jimmy McGovern has declared:

> 'I would rather be confused for 10 minutes, than bored for five seconds.'

### The opposite of listening is waiting

Something else that people actually do in conversations is to wait rather than listen. They are waiting for an opportunity to get in and to get their own point across. Real conversations are not formal question and answer sessions with the participants politely waiting for each other to finish their sentences. In the previously mentioned *Screenwipe*, Russell T Davies says:

> 'When you're writing dialogue, it's actually two monologues that just connect sometimes.'

Rib Davis points out that every character in any conversation has their own personal agenda. He suggests as an exercise, writing two separate short conversations between two characters, A and B. In the first, character A has a clear agenda and is anxious to make a point. In the second, character B clearly has something on their mind. Now write a third conversation between character A and character B attempting to merge the two previous conversations. The result may make no sense, but it is possible that you will end up with something that replicates a real conversation where there is more than one topic, where there is a conflict of interest, where there is the untidiness of natural speech and where there is drama.

### Information is boring

Characters telling each other things they already know as a means of conveying information to the audience should be avoided at all costs, as should other unsubtle, verbal 'clues'. Russell T Davies deplores lines like 'Well you would say that, being my brother' or 'Happy wedding day, sis'. As he says, 'Who calls their sister, "sis"?'

Good writing gives the audience information without making them aware they are being given information. Exposition can be hidden within conflict or disguised by comedy. In the first episode of *Cheers*, Diane is explaining at length to Sam, the barman, (and to the audience) that she and her fiancé, Sumner, are colleagues at the university where she is his teaching assistant and he is Professor of World Literature. He proposed to her, while she was reading her copy of Yeats, by proclaiming 'Come live with me, and be my love. And we will some new pleasures prove'. When told:

> That's Donne.

Sam replies:

> I certainly hope so.

While Diane has been talking, Sam has been opening a bottle of champagne and is clearly unimpressed and bored by what she has been telling him, as his comment implies. Thus, Diane's back-story is entertainingly filtered to the audience through Sam's indifference to it. A similar technique is used later in the same episode when the waitress, Carla, tells a bemused Diane about an exploit from Sam's professional baseball career.

### Subtext

Don't write on the nose, allowing characters to state the obvious or to hold nothing back. In real life people rarely express how they really feel or what they really think. We get a sense of their true feelings behind what they are actually saying or doing. It should be the same in drama, where the contrast between what a character is saying and what they are doing is what engages the audience. It is the subtext in a scene, which conveys to the audience what it is really about, the actual meaning lying behind the apparent surface meaning. Ray Frensham describes subtext as 'what is being communicated beneath the text lines or action; the real meaning being conveyed, the real intent (conscious or unconscious) of the character. For the writer, subtext expresses the hidden agenda of a character.' There is a scene in *Shameless*, where Frank Gallagher is scathingly running down his wife to Steve, his daughter Fiona's new boyfriend, relating how she abandoned him and all her children. It is clear to the audience from the little that Fiona has to say in the scene and from what she doesn't say that she has a different opinion of her mother's behaviour, but she is not expressing it. As Paul Abbott puts it, 'loving her mother, she is deliberately not starting the row she knows she can't win'.

Screenwriter and academic, Craig Batty, gives his screenwriting students a helpful dialogue exercise, which encourages the use of subtext. A couple have been on a first date, which seems to have gone well. However, neither of them is sure how the other feels about them or the evening. They leave the restaurant and approach the parked car of one of them. Write a conversation between them, which is seemingly about the car, but is actually about whether they are going to see each other again or perhaps go further this evening . . .

# 14 Audience expectations: formats and genres

Some television audiences will be more demanding than others, but they are all very sophisticated. Regular television viewers watch a lot of television and are very media literate. If you are going to satisfy those viewers, then you will need to understand the ways in which different kinds of programmes work and learn to master their codes and conventions.

## What's the concept?

Long-running television series appeal to audiences and appeal to broadcasters. Any idea submitted will be judged not only on its potential to deliver an audience but on its ability to generate a number of series and a large number of varied episodes.

The most successful series and the series that last longest are those which have a strong concept. This is the basic premise of the show, the fundamental idea or set of ideas at its core, the foundation on which everything else sits. The concept suggests theme, dictates characters and story and governs tone and humour. A show with a strong concept is an identifiable 'brand' that audiences will return to again and again and which can travel into other television markets. The concept of some shows is actually expressed in the title: *Waking the Dead, Desperate Housewives, Lost, Mad Men, Criminal Justice.*

A **high concept** show is one whose premise can be simply communicated in a single phrase or sentence. 'A single father takes a job as a live-in domestic for a working mother' *(The Upper Hand)*. 'A writer of mystery novels uses her craft to solve murders' *(Murder, She Wrote)*. 'A scientist is exposed to radiation and mutates into a green monster whenever he experiences rage' *(The Incredible Hulk)*. All of these shows, incidentally, clocked up multiple seasons and crossed borders.

When developing a new show, it is important to find, define and refine the concept. What do you want to say? What is your angle? What makes this show unique? Once the concept is established, you will know what is right and wrong for your series in terms of the characters and the stories. *The Sopranos, Guardian* TV critics' 'greatest TV drama ever made' (22 February 2011), embodies in its concept a different take on American 'family values' when the 'family' is the mob in an era of diminished expectations. Chris Albrecht, HBO's former president of original programming, recalls in *Vanity Fair* (April 2007) that the show was about a guy with typical mid-life problems:

'He's anxious; he's depressed; he starts to see a therapist because he's searching for the meaning of his own life. I thought: The only difference between him and everybody I know is he's the don of New Jersey. So, to me, the Mafia part was sort of the tickle for why you watched. The reason you stayed was because of the resonance and relatability of all that other stuff.'

If a show has a strong concept, then whenever new writers come onto it or new producers take it over, they will have no problem contributing to it and evolving it, but still delivering what its audience expects. In this way a team-written show like *Frasier* can have a 'voice' that is just as distinctive as a single-authored show like *One Foot in the Grave*.

Fifty years after it started, *Coronation Street* is still recognisably the same show at its core that Tony Warren created in 1960. For 25 years *EastEnders* has consistently been about the Blitz spirit. As John Yorke describes it, 'No matter what life throws at you, you don't give up, you don't surrender, you fight back'. Any writer working on either of these shows would instinctively know what is appropriate for each of them and that is because they each have a very strong and distinctive concept. They are about something.

A concept does not have to be complex or extraordinary to ensure success or sustainability. What could be simpler than 'Six friends who hang out at a coffee shop'? Yet *Friends* lasted for 10 seasons.

## Writing for different formats and genres

When Julian and I set up the De Montfort Television Scriptwriting MA, we designed it so that the students would have the experience of writing for a number of different television formats and genres. Outside their 'comfort zone', many students have discovered an aptitude and enthusiasm for areas of writing they wouldn't previously have considered. One, who joined the course specifically to write sitcom, has become a successful drama series writer; another, having previously only focused on issue-based serious drama, really enjoyed writing a sitcom on the course and her first commission after graduating was a comedy-drama series for Hat Trick.

It is worth trying to develop ideas for different television audiences. You may surprise yourself with what you gain from the experience!

## Drama series

Drama series are a popular and essential component of the TV schedules, particularly on the mainstream channels. They consistently deliver ratings to broadcasters and entertainment to loyal audiences. There is a tendency now for most series to contain a serial element, something imported from the soaps, but the 'story of the week' is still paramount and, unlike in a serial, the characters don't change. What does change though is their knowledge – Inspector Morse knows more at the end of an episode than he did at the beginning, but he is not changed by his experience.

Successful shows as diverse as *Life on Mars, Heartbeat, The West Wing, Spooks, House, Dexter, Inspector Morse* and *CSI* have these elements in common which provide them with predictability.

- They have the same characters – usually an ensemble.
- There is a plot that resolves every week.
- There is a clear and renewable story engine.
- They are always in the same location.
- There are guest characters (the antagonists, whose stories often resonate with the main characters' stories).
- They are about something – in other words, they are concept driven.

John Yorke stresses above all that mainstream drama series are 'feel-good telly' – '*Shameless* and *The Waltons* are both the same, they make you feel good at the end.' We empathise with the characters and we care about them. They invoke the concept of family or gang. The gang unites to solve the problem of the week. In *Life on Mars*, Sam Tyler and Gene Hunt disagree, then they go on a journey and realise they can learn from each other. They are opposites, but they reconcile their differences and the problem is solved. However, the reset button is pressed at the end of each episode and they disagree again. They forget that they got on, so they can go through the same journey again next week.

Such dramas offer reassurance to the viewer. Whatever life throws at them, the characters fight back and everything always comes right in the end. They offer hope. John Yorke points out that life is tough and that the viewer doesn't want to feel worse at the end of the programme than they did at the beginning. If they don't feel better at the end, they won't come back.

John Yorke maintains that all series are about the concept of *family*. The family must survive and their home must be defended. The enemy is without. Whether it's in *Shameless* or *Casualty*, the characters (the 'family') are protecting their home. John says:

> 'In the first episode of *ER*, every single story is telling you how important that precinct is and how they are protecting it. The gang comes together and defends the home. Writers have to define their concept of home. We have to aspire to be there – we want to be in the Gallaghers' front room in *Shameless*.'

The holy grail for drama commissioners is the show that captures the spirit of the times we live in. Shows like *Shameless*, *Minder* and *Auf Wiedersehen, Pet* captured a moment of social change and reflected it back to the audience.

### *The bottom line*

Shows are primarily based in one location, because they are cheaper to produce. (In the past a show like *Alias Smith and Jones* or *Quantum Leap* could afford to go somewhere different every episode.) For the same reason episodes are often set within one day or one shift and night shoots are used sparingly.

*Hotel Babylon* was a show that worked particularly well for its audience and the broadcaster. It had high production values and an attractive range of regular characters. However, it was relatively inexpensive to produce as all the drama could take place within the precinct itself – a five star luxury hotel. Each week an endless supply of hotel guests could provide interesting stories, which did not require location shooting or time-consuming action sequences. Stylishly shot and very easy on the eye, it was cost-effective, but importantly it didn't look cheap. As the downward pressure on budgets continues to influence drama production, there will be an increasing demand for shows like this.

### *Cops, docs and lawyers*

> 'Television . . . is rigidly governed by the clock, there is no time to sit around . . . Characters must be presented with one crisis after another – preferably more than any normal mortal or group of mortals could ever handle in a single day . . . the need to sustain a series . . . explains why television characters so often work in the medical, police, detective, and law fields. In these fields, you don't have to go looking for adventure, you just show up for work.'
>
> *Howard Suber:* The Power of Film *(2006), Michael Wiese Productions*

From *Dixon of Dock Green, Emergency Ward 10* and *Perry Mason* to *The Bill, Casualty* and *Silk*, crime, medical and legal dramas have always dominated the schedules. The audience can relate to them and they are natural arenas for drama and crisis – life and death situations are part of the territory. They also contain plenty of opportunities for characters genuinely to be heroic, saving, protecting and defending lives. Dramas (and audiences) need heroes.

Barbara Machin says that writers can use a crime drama as a Trojan horse to tell the stories that really interest them. She adds that though a formula can strangle creativity, a strong template that makes the rules can be liberating for the writer. *Waking the Dead* needed to excavate the past and the use of flashbacks became an important aspect of the narrative style. In some of her first stories Barbara began to push the use of flashbacks beyond simply recounting the history of the case. Memory is of course subjective and so the flashbacks of an unreliable narrator, and thus many points of view, could be used to create thrilling twists and turns before the truth was finally revealed. Also flash-*forwards* can be used to create imagined versions of what might have happened. Thus, a primarily naturalistic drama form appropriately adopted more stylistic techniques to dramatise the actual process of crime solving.

Peter Berry was the writer of *Prime Suspect VI: The Last Witness*. While stressing that a story of the writer's choice can't be imposed from the outside, always having to be about the regular characters, he was able to write a powerful drama on a subject that really attracted him. It was about asylum seekers and the murderous consequences of war crimes committed in Bosnia. A subject he had been keen to write about, he knew it was not the kind of story that would normally ever find its way onto primetime ITV. Not only was it very dark, but it was principally about 'foreigners' and much of it was not set on the familiar streets of Britain. Telling the story as a *Prime Suspect*, as a case for Jane Tennison, brought it a huge mainstream audience of 12 million viewers and four BAFTA nominations.

Similarly, Tony Marchant talks about 'smuggling' his writing passions into the conventions of a popular Sunday night legal drama. *Garrow's Law* is a successful period series with gripping courtroom scenes and plenty of personal and professional jeopardy for its appealing leading character. In William Garrow, Marchant was drawn to a historical figure, who was an 'outsider' to the legal system, who was 'trying to overturn the status quo' in order for defendants to receive a fair trial. True stories like the case of the Zong (133 slaves thrown overboard a ship), told through 'the reversals and revelations, last minute interventions and the suspense of the judgement' of a compelling court case, reach a much wider audience than a TV documentary could.

In *Subverting the Formula*, a 2002 article for *ScriptWriter* magazine (www.twelvepoint.com), Matthew Friday compares the pilot episodes of seven different crime dramas. Unsurprisingly, he decides that the key to success lies in well-drawn, complex characters, rather than plot:

> 'This explains why we watch the same drama over and over again. Knowing what happens next is less important than the kick we get out of sharing the world of the characters. Once this is understood you'll stop creating your police dramas around drug heists and international porn rings and base it around complex, multifaceted characters driven by the need to realise goals and aspirations and achieve some kind of happiness.'

He concludes with the following advice regarding the **pilot episode**.

- **The pilot.** Everything is new to the audience except a sense of familiarity. You have to capture the feel of the whole series without being compelled to tell every character's story.
- **The bright idea.** Don't waste your time creating something no one's going to buy.
- **The premise.** Three different styles: ensemble police stations, specialist teams within the police, the detective double act. Do your research. See what's being commissioned.
- **Demographic.** Know your audience and the channels on which the programme is likely to be shown since this dictates content and style.
- **Characters.** Your main character should preferably be new to the environment. Create strong supporting characters with opposing viewpoints.
- **Exploit the office environment.** Have arguments with senior staff up against the drinks machine, not on Dartmoor in a storm at night. Remember how expensive drama is, especially on location and at night.
- **Act One.** Bring your new character into a world that appears to be going about business as usual. But this case is the 'big one' with resources stretched to the limit and careers on the line. Do whatever you have to do to give this pilot major impact.
- **Act Two.** Plenty of subplots and minor characters. Remember the social setting. Follow through with the mystery set up in Act One. Audiences love a challenge.
- **Act Three.** Have the new character in danger that they seem unlikely to overcome and then rescue them at the last minute.
- **Catching the audience.** Keep the carrot in front of the audience. Hint at what is to come. Reward the audience for watching.

### *Twisting the familiar*

There is always a balance between following a formula that is tried and tested (and reassuringly familiar to the audience) and doing something entertainingly different with it. A study of a wide cross-section of shows will identify common codes and conventions. The challenge for the writer in a pilot episode is to play on audience expectations by occasionally breaking the rules and twisting the familiar. Nevertheless, it is dangerous to break the rules without knowing what they are – the commissioners and the audience will be very familiar with them.

It is almost impossible to come up with an idea for a drama series that hasn't been seen before. If it hasn't been done before, there is often a good reason. I have encountered a number of series ideas that wouldn't work because they lacked a clear and renewable 'story engine' – a series about ambulance drivers (the guest stories were unresolved once the patients were delivered to hospital); a mountain rescue team (every episode the same story); building site health and safety inspectors (limited story potential).

Sometimes familiar elements from different genres can be successfully combined. There was nothing in *Desperate Housewives*, originally pitched as *'Knot's Landing* meets *American Beauty'*, that the audience hadn't seen before. However, they hadn't seen those elements in the same show. By cleverly mixing television genres (soap, sitcom, mystery etc.), Marc Cherry created something entirely new.

Sometimes familiar territory can be approached from an unfamiliar angle to produce a successful drama series. Crime detection dramas were given a new twist when forensic teams, previously only seen in the background, became the protagonists of their own shows. *Silent*

*Witness* has been running for 15 years and the *CSI* franchise is popular all over the world.

---

## Writing for existing drama series

It goes without saying that if you want to write for an existing series, a detailed knowledge of the show in question is essential. If you are not a regular viewer, then do your research. If you approach the writing of an episode for a particular series as a stepping stone to something else, then you won't succeed. The secret of success is to fall in love with every single character you are writing for.

Different series will have different house rules that will need to be adhered to. Commissioned writers will receive series 'bibles' and guidelines that will contain the necessary information. However, all series will demand stories that primarily involve and impact on the regular characters. Guest characters will often be responsible for introducing plots and subplots, but they must not be allowed to dominate the proceedings. Remember that the audience is tuning in to spend time with the regular characters, not with the guests. They want to see how they are going to solve the problems that are presented to them and, thus, they should have most at stake. The best episodes reveal new things about the regulars through their encounters with the guests.

---

## Soaps

Soap opera is the most watched form of drama on British television and the area where most television writers get their first professional experience. Paul Abbott (*Coronation Street*), Jimmy McGovern (*Brookside*), Ashley Pharoah and Tony Jordan (*EastEnders*) all learned their craft writing for the soaps. However, it is not an area for the faint-hearted. Deadlines are tight and writers need to be very disciplined in their approach, if they are going to survive.

There are fewer individual soaps than there used to be and, particularly with the demise of less high-profile shows like the revived *Crossroads* and Channel 5's *Family Affairs*, less opportunities for inexperienced writers to be commissioned.

*Coronation Street, EastEnders* and *Hollyoaks* all run shadow schemes for new writers who have impressed their script departments with work they have submitted. Selected writers are given the opportunity to write a shadow episode under the same conditions and to the same deadlines as a commissioned writer. What they are looking for is not only the ability of the writer to write with the voice of the show and to deliver a professional script, but also to put something of themselves into their work and to make it distinctive. Although the episode story they are given cannot be changed, how it is shaped and how it is told is in the hands of the writer.

An understanding of the characters' motivations is a crucial prerequisite for a successful script. It is vital for any aspiring soap writer to do their homework, to watch the show, to know the show and, ideally, to be passionate about it. A soap episode invariably contains an A, a B and a C storyline. A shadow episode will demonstrate the writer's ability to handle the three storylines and to weave them together for maximum dramatic effect. There may be unifying themes or contrasting tones in the different story strands that can be exploited. In *Hollyoaks*, for instance, the C storyline often provides comic relief, if the A storyline is particularly heavy.

If a writer is fortunate enough to be taken on after writing a shadow episode, they will soon learn that writing for television is a process of collaboration and compromise. It will take more than raw writing talent to ensure survival. In 'Writing for the Soaps', a 2008 article for *ScriptWriter* magazine (www.twelvepoint.com), Yvonne Grace gives the following advice.

- **Have strong opinions about the characters** – don't be a shrinking violet.

- **Have strong story ideas** – explore the characters involved and reveal something interesting about them to your audience.

- **Familiarise yourself with the script team** – especially the key players.

- **Find out as much as you can about the production process** – if you understand something of the pressures your script editor may be under to deliver your script to deadline, it'll go a long way to creating a harmonious partnership and that editor will want to work with you again.

- **Be positive and helpful to work with** – script editors are your friends. Being open-minded to script changes, collaborative in your approach to your writing task and even saying yes and doing the rewrites without having a mini-breakdown about the time-frame they have given you, will ensure you are invited back again.

- **Embrace the fast turnaround and keep at it** – soap writing becomes easier with practice.

- **Be organised** – there is never enough time but you have to work within the deadlines you are given.

- **Be collaborative** – show respect and listen to the opinions of your fellow writers.

*Doctors* also runs a shadow scheme in order to assess a new writer's suitability for the show. Each episode does contain some serial elements, but it also includes a self-contained story. This makes it an attractive proposition, compared to a soap, as the writer is invited to pitch their own ideas. They can introduce their own characters and tell their own story, which means that up to 70% of the episode can be theirs. However, developing ideas for *Doctors* can be hard, as it is difficult to come up with something that hasn't been done before.

With a running time of approximately 25 minutes, a typical *Doctors* episode contains two stories, one for a guest character and one for a member of the regular cast, told in five acts of about five to six minutes in length.

## Singles

In the past a writer's introduction to writing for television was likely to be a commission for a single play. However, today's television schedules need returning series and serials – there is little or no demand for single dramas. They are perceived as difficult to schedule, compared to series where the audience know what to expect and can engage with familiar characters.

### Clocking Off *and* The Street

Some writers, notably Paul Abbott and Jimmy McGovern, have found ingenious solutions to this problem. Paul Abbott's series *Clocking Off* set in Mackintosh Textiles was in effect an anthology of single plays, each individual story being about a character who worked in the factory. Nevertheless, it had the feel of a conventional series. There was a sense of community and a cast of regular characters for the audience, but as one would be the focus for each episode, the others would fade into the background.

Jimmy McGovern's award-winning series *The Street* similarly presented an anthology of single dramas with a location and some characters in common. McGovern worked with a number of writers, many of whom were new to television, to tell the compelling and unusual stories of the residents of an ordinary street.

---

### Write what you know

'I do mine my own life for material. It gives it more authenticity, especially when you're surprised by how you feel. When you put those emotions into a script, they have the smack of authenticity. It endows a script with so much more richness if it comes from your own life.'
*Jimmy McGovern* (The Street, *BBC Press Pack 2007*)

'Even though it's a Mob show, *The Sopranos* is based on members of my family. It's about as personal as you can get.'
*David Chase* (Vanity Fair, *April 2007*)

---

Jimmy McGovern has followed up *The Street* with *Accused*, where each episode tells the story of a different character awaiting their verdict in court. He has also executive produced *Moving On*, a BBC 1 daytime series of single dramas all written by new writers and all linked by one central theme – moving on in life after dealing with contemporary issues.

Launching the first series of *The Street*, John Yorke referred to it as a 'modern play for today'. There is clearly a future for single plays, if attractive ways can be found to deliver them to a drama audience more accustomed to a diet of returning series.

## TV movies

While the single dramas featured in *Moving On* and *The Street* are respectively 45 and 60 minutes in length, there are also occasionally 90-minute single dramas, the equivalent of low budget feature films. Some of these (from Channel 4's *My Beautiful Laundrette* to the BBC's *Billy Elliot*), though originally developed for the small screen, have had a theatrical release before being screened on television.

Because of the cost of such projects, they are often co-productions between television companies and other interested parties. Various different factors will determine whether they ever get off the ground, often related to the level of acting and directing talent that they can attract in the initial stages.

Completely original stories are a rarity. Just as Hollywood has always played it safe, preferring to tell fictional stories that have already succeeded in pleasing an audience – it is estimated that well over 75% of films are adaptations – or stories based on facts that are familiar to the audience, television is no different. While recent BBC1 examples of literary adaptations include *The 39 Steps* and *The Turn of the Screw*, BBC4 has favoured factually based films.

This is quite understandable. As Kate Harwood, BBC Controller, Series & Serials, points out in an interview for www.twelvepoint.com:

'Singles have to make an impact in the schedule otherwise there's no point, people aren't actually going to find them. They need to have something behind them.'

They need to hook an audience.

## Factual drama

A number of recent TV films have been based on the lives or experiences of real people: from *Margaret Thatcher: The Long Walk to Finchley*, *Lennon Naked* and *Enid*, *Margot* and *Gracie* (Blyton, Fonteyn and Fields) on the BBC to *The Government Inspector* (Dr David Kelly), *The Shooting of Thomas Hurndall* and *Mo* (Mowlam) on Channel 4.

Tony Marchant's *The Mark of Cain*, though a work of fiction, was based on extensive research into the behaviour and experiences of young British soldiers in Iraq. He wanted to write about the subject after reading about the abuse of Iraqi prisoners by British 'boys', sufficiently unfazed by what they had done to be able to take their incriminating photos to be developed at a local photo shop (who notified the police). Marchant says:

> 'If you're going to find a way into a subject like this, then you need to find something universal and for me what this was ultimately about was about friendship between two 18-year-old boys. It was about a rite of passage that took place in an extraordinary context – the Iraq War.'

Finding a way into a subject that can make it into an involving drama for an audience is always a challenge for a writer. Simply presenting the facts is not an option. When Michael Eaton was writing his TV film *Shipman*, he knew that the GP himself, who had never explained his motives and who never 'changed' as central characters have to do, could not be his focus. He told the story from the perspective of Stan Egerton, the dogged detective inspector, whose personal journey forced him to 'think the unthinkable' and, literally in his last case before retirement, to investigate this 'pillar of the community'.

---

### A story of envy and revenge

Mozart was a genius. He was born a genius and he died a genius. As a character he didn't change and, in any event, a genius is not a character with whom an audience can readily identify. Peter Shaffer's way into this subject was through Salieri, the mediocre and bitter court composer, whose career was eclipsed by the brilliant and vulgar upstart. *Amadeus,* a powerful story of envy and revenge, won eight Academy Awards. A straightforward life story of Mozart would not have been so compelling.

---

### *Why you should write a TV film*

The chances of a new writer receiving a commission for a TV film are extremely remote. However, it is not impossible – BBC Films' *The Theory of Flight,* starring Kenneth Branagh and Helena Bonham Carter and directed by Paul Greengrass, was Richard Hawkins' first commission. Nevertheless, any writer serious about breaking into television should have a feature length drama in their portfolio.

It will show the reader your original voice as a writer. It will demonstrate your ability to introduce an audience to a specific world, to set up characters and through an involving story to take them on a journey to a satisfying conclusion. You may not be able to sell it, but more importantly it may sell you. Some years ago a student of mine was invited to join the writing team on *Emmerdale* on the strength of an unproduced film script she had submitted.

Tim Bevan, co-founder and co-chairman of Working Title Films, was asked at the London Screenwriters' Festival what he looked for in screenplays. He replied, 'Good stories, good characters, good emotions.' Where many speculative TV film scripts fall down is on the third of these – emotion. If you are going to engage an audience for 90 minutes or longer, then there has to be a big emotional pay-off. There has to be more at stake, there have to be bigger 'moments', there have to be more significant consequences than in the average episode of a TV series.

Characters in films have to change and it is the significance of those changes that has the power to move the audience. Ray Frensham states that it is the '*transformation and growth*' of the characters, which enables them finally to overcome the obstacles in their path and to reach their goal.

Remember that the most effective screenplays are those you write with passion and with emotions that come from your own life.

## Situation comedy

Situation comedy (sitcom) series have much in common with drama series. From *I Love Lucy* to *The IT Crowd*, they feature a regular group of characters in a specific setting with a self-contained story in each episode. Not only do the characters never change, but whatever journeys they go on they always end up where they started – the status quo is always maintained.

Although they are designed to provide laughs, it is important that they are approached in the same way as any other form of drama. As Steven Moffat, creator of *Coupling*, says:

'You can't cheat with character or cheat with plot, just because it's a comedy.'

You should write the drama, making it peak into moments of laughter. He says that 'the ideal sitcom gag' is when you take something from your own life and 'sharpen the moment into a joke', adding that importing 'jokes' or 'wisecracks' never works. The humour should stem organically from the characters and the situations.

Whereas dramas tend to be about the heroic exploits of extraordinary people or about ordinary people called upon to do extraordinary deeds, sitcoms are about the minutiae of everyday life of ordinary people. Thus, sitcoms more closely mirror the lives of their audience and the laughter is the laughter of recognition.

*Coupling* was closely modelled on Moffat's own life with his wife, Sue – the central couple were even called Steve and Susan and the exteriors were actually filmed at his own house in West London. Similarly, the movie characters Richard Curtis creates for Hugh Grant are always versions of himself. This doesn't mean that all successful comedy writing should be autobiographical, but the more of yourself and your own experience you can base it on the more effective it will be. David Renwick was still in his thirties when he created *One Foot in the Grave*, but he was able to put all his own irritations and frustrations with modern life into the character of Victor Meldrew.

### The format

In spite of its title, situation comedy is actually character comedy. Some writers mistakenly assume that all they have to do is to come up with a situation or setting that hasn't been tried before (virtually impossible), as if the comedy is all about the situation. In fact the situation, whatever it is, is simply the framework that holds the characters together. The comedy comes from the situations that the characters get themselves into (think of Larry David in *Curb Your Enthusiasm*) and from the relationships they have with each other.

The centres of action in a sitcom are limited so where your series takes place needs to be carefully considered. Two or three basic sets is the norm and Paul Mayhew Archer, co-writer of the *Vicar of Dibley*, advises that the more characters you have, the fewer the centres of action there should be. In *Dad's Army* most of the action is in the hall, in *Cheers* most of the action is in the bar – we don't tend to follow the characters home, so the focus of the shows is always clear and simple.

I was once pitched an idea about a girl employed as a temp; in each episode she was sent to a different job in a different office. This wouldn't work as a sitcom. In each episode the audience would be introduced to a new set of characters and each episode would require a different setting, which would be very costly. If the focus had been the temping agency itself where most of the regular characters worked and we rarely, if ever, visited the clients' offices, then it would have had more potential. The principal centre of action for *Taxi* is the garage of the Sunshine Cab Company presided over by Danny DeVito's head dispatcher, not out on the road with the drivers.

Paul Mayhew Archer also stresses that it is important to consider what your show is *really* about. Successful shows need to be about *us* – their appeal should be universal. *Steptoe and Son* isn't just about rag and bone men; it's about parents and children. *Porridge* isn't about prison; it's about innocence and experience.

## Sitcom characters

Audiences have great affection for their favourite characters in sitcoms and the most popular shows will bear far more repeat viewings and will shift far more DVDs than the most popular dramas. The characters are larger than life, but still recognisably drawn from life. They are not caricatures. Basil Fawlty, David Brent, Edmund Blackadder and Alan Partridge are all monsters and their behaviour can be way over the top, but we can understand what motivates them and share their frustrations.

> 'Audiences don't laugh at scripts, they laugh at people.'
> *David Renwick (Media Guardian, 22 March 1999)*
>
> 'What makes most TV a hit is if audiences want these people back in their house.'
> *Maurice Gran (Media Guardian, 20 September 1999)*

Audiences are attracted to triers, characters who are striving for something, who are willing to have a go. Passive characters are less interesting and can be boring. Although characters in sitcoms rarely achieve their goals – if they did it would be a different show next week – we admire them for their determination. In their different ways and in their different worlds, both Del Boy and Joey always bounce back from their disappointments and remain optimistic.

Writer Guy Meredith recommends making use of the seven deadly sins when creating comic characters, in order to avoid what he calls 'pale protagonist syndrome'. Although sloth may not be particularly helpful, the others – pride, greed, lust, envy, gluttony and anger – are all powerful emotions that can not only motivate characters' behaviour and get them into comic situations, but also connect them with the audience. There are not many of the seven deadly sins that haven't got Frasier Crane or Edmund Blackadder into trouble.

Characters in sitcoms are trapped and, much as they may want to, they are unable to escape. In *Porridge*, they are literally locked up together, but whether it is the family they are born into or the office where they are obliged to work, they are forced to relate to other people. Blood ties are very useful in sitcoms as a means of keeping incompatible characters together and providing opportunities for dramatic conflict and comic juxtapositions. Harold Steptoe can't leave his father, because he's his father. *Birds of a Feather*'s Sharon and Tracey would be unlikely to stick together, if they were not sisters. Frasier has no choice but to share his new apartment with his father, who can no longer live on his own.

Sitcoms are about relationships, it is not enough to assemble a random bunch of amusing characters in a given situation and expect it to work. We don't tune in to *The Office* to watch the characters doing their jobs, but to see how they relate to each other – Tim's petty squabbles with Gareth, Tim's little chats with Dawn, Tim's mixture of humouring and irritation in his dealings with his boss. Hierarchies are always useful as characters will behave differently according to the status of those they are with.

Simon Nye, creator of *Men Behaving Badly*, thinks that 'drama focuses on antagonisms whereas comedy is more interested in bonds and friendships, albeit with superficial hilarious antagonisms.' Shaun O'Riordan always stressed the importance of 'charm' in comedy and he was talking about the same thing. This is why audiences warm to their favourite sitcoms. Of course comedy can be cruel, but both the final episodes of *Blackadder Goes Forth* and of

*The Office* – the 'Christmas Special' – are as much about 'bonds and friendships' as any episode of *Friends* or *Gavin & Stacey*.

> 'For me, situation comedy is something of a misnomer because character is the core element. Everything revolves around character. Once you have created convincing comic characters you find that, somehow, they manage to create their own world. This world may be surreal, even bizarre, but whatever form it takes it will allow the characters to bloom.
>
> 'The "situation" stems from character. Beyond that I can offer no "rules", other than work as hard as possible to get the script right, cast great actors and don't work with lemons.'
> *Andy Hamilton* (Drop the Dead Donkey, Outnumbered)

### The plot

A sitcom episode needs a strong plot – it needs to be 'about' something. By the end of the first scene, it should be clear to the audience what the story is about. Alongside the A story, there will usually be a B story and a C story (sometimes no more than a running gag) and in this way you can ensure that all your characters are involved. In the best-written episodes the A and B stories will overlap towards the end – it is very satisfying when an element in one story can be used to solve the problem in the other story, particularly when the audience hasn't previously made the connection.

In the *Frasier* episode 'You Scratch My Book' referred to earlier, Frasier forces Niles to stop pretending Daphne's investments are rising, (the B story), accusing him of 'misleading a woman for his 'own selfish gain'. However, Niles gets his own back, reproaching him for being equally dishonest to Honey Snow, (the A story), and Frasier concedes he is going to have to tell her he can't write the foreword to her book. The C story, Niles selling raffle tickets in the first scene 'to support Maris's little opera group' is paid off at the end when their lead soprano turns up to perform 'The Ride of the Valkyries' (the first prize).

> 'When I started writing sitcoms I thought it was all about creating interesting characters – wind them up and listen to them chat amusingly. But I've come to realise that an efficient, vibrant plot is vital. It may be irrelevant but my first sitcoms had perhaps seven scenes, now they are more likely to have 20.'
> *Simon Nye*

The best stories put the characters under pressure, because it's when they're under pressure that their behaviour becomes most extreme and most funny – think of Basil Fawlty in any episode of *Fawlty Towers*. Paul Mayhew Archer advises:

> 'Make life more and more problematical for your characters – and just when they think they've solved the problem . . . make it worse.'

The best stories are character driven, not plot driven. The characters should always get themselves into trouble, rather than having trouble thrust upon them. In other words, if a character is going to slip on a banana skin, it is better if somehow or other they are responsible for the banana skin being there in the first place.

> **Read *Just William***
>
> 'I said to Ian La Frenais, "Plotting is so difficult" and he said "Read *Just William*. Best comedy plotting in the world." Richmal Crompton's stories are beautifully crafted comedies.'
> *Laurence Marks*

## Comedy-drama

'It's a comedy-drama' used to be the excuse offered for a comedy that wasn't very comic or a drama that wasn't very dramatic. However, as more half-hour comedies started to be produced without a studio audience (e.g. *Shine on Harvey Moon* in 1982) and more one-hour dramas started to be produced by comedy producers and comedy writers (e.g. *Auf Wiedersehen, Pet* in 1983), the term began to be used to describe a wide variety of successful sitcoms and drama series.

In general terms, 30-minute comedy-dramas tend to be *comedies* with strong dramatic serial elements (*Gavin & Stacy, Entourage*), while 60-minute comedy-dramas tend to be *dramas* with strong elements of humour (*Shameless, Desperate Housewives*). Although there are always exceptions, this means that 30-minute shows should be submitted to comedy departments and 60-minute shows should be submitted to drama departments.

If you are developing an idea for a 30-minute comedy, you need to consider whether it is going to be a traditional sitcom (which may or may not be shot in front of a studio audience) or whether it should be a single-camera comedy-drama. While a sitcom will demand a steady stream of laughs and comic situations, a comedy-drama will require a stronger emphasis on story and character development and will be less reliant on gags. Many are romantic comedies.

A 60-minute comedy-drama will need a lot of story to keep the audience watching – there is always a lot at stake for a number of different people in an episode of *Shameless* – and cannot be approached as if it is simply a longer version of a sitcom. It is often a question of tone or the manner in which it is presented that makes a show a comedy-drama, rather than its subject matter.

## Children's television

This book has stressed the importance of connecting with the television audience and taking it into account at every stage of the writing process. It is particularly important when writing for children to know exactly which distinct children's audience you are writing for, to be aware of the stages of development of that particular age group and to understand what is appropriate for them. When writer/producer Jocelyn Stevenson, whose experience ranges from *Sesame Street* to *Bob the Builder*, teaches the basics of writing for pre-school children, her focus is always on the different stages of child development.

Guy Hallifax explains, in *ScriptWriter* magazine, that the children's audience is divided by commissioners and schedulers into age groups that represent average levels of intelligence, education and experience. These are roughly 2–5, 6–8 and 9–11 years. Above that is designated as family programming. Children's channels set their own parameters. While the remit of CBeebies is to encourage learning through play for children under 6, the remit of CBBC is to provide a wide range of high-quality distinctive content for 6–12 year olds. There is a huge difference, for instance, in the capabilities and interests of a 6 year old and a 12 year old. This makes writing for children particularly challenging.

### Writing for pre-school children's series

My first experience of working in television was writing scripts and stories for *Play School*. Having a background in children's theatre, I knew something about how to communicate with the target audience for the show. However, it was essential to watch as many episodes as I could and to talk to the parents of children who watched it regularly in order to appreciate how this particular show worked and how to meet its audience's expectations. While predictability is a common element of adult drama series, it is a crucial element of series for very young children.

Writers on children's series will receive guidelines and bibles, as comprehensive as those for any adult series. The Writers Bible for *Bob the Builder* (aimed at 2–5 year olds) has as many pages as the one for *Casualty*! Each 10-minute episode is as tightly structured as any sitcom, with an A and a B plot and crucial turning points at key moments. The stories always involve friends helping friends out of trouble, solving problems and providing shoulders to lean on – endorsing Simon Nye's observation that comedy focuses on 'bonds and friendships'.

There are always four 'key' questions that need to be answered about an episode of a pre-school series.

- Whose story is it?
- What's their goal?

- What do they risk? (i.e. Where's the jeopardy?)
- What do they learn?

The 10-minute stories for *Thomas & Friends* are character-led and structured in three acts and are always about something. In Act One the main character's goal is revealed and they commit to a course of action, which is usually ill-guided. In Act Two the situation gets worse and worse and worse until the 'Oh my god!' moment. In Act Three the main character realises what they have done and, often with the help of their friends, finally puts it right. All the stories have an uplifting quality – this is a world where 'admitting you are scared means you are brave after all'.

The key to writing for very young children is **simplicity** and **clarity**; muddle must be avoided. Off-screen events do not work for this audience; they have to **see** the action.

### *Programme ideas*

When submitting a programme proposal for very young children, it is better to send in a page outline than a script. It is the concept that will be assessed, rather than your writing skills. Shows that go into production will have long runs and will always have a writing team attached to them. Not only will a proposal be judged on its ability to generate several long-running series, but also on what HIT Entertainment calls 'extendibility'. It has to be able to extend beyond the broadcast platform and to be easily merchandised and licensed.

While Captain Pugwash was a cardboard cut-out and Bagpuss was a 'saggy old cloth cat', today's sophisticated CGI animation and high production values mean that many programmes cost more to make than they can earn from TV broadcasts alone. They need to become brands with the ability to sell toys and DVDs and lunch-boxes.

Whereas other television markets may not be taken into account when home-grown drama is being developed, overseas sales are a very important part of the children's animation economy and foreign-language versions need to be considered at all stages of the production. For instance, text on screen – on signs or posters etc. – needs to be avoided. All the elements of a story need to be thought about carefully, as Guy Hallifax points out for example: 'Cats are universally recognised and understood by children, but hedgehogs aren't.'

It is not only in terms of merchandising potential that programme proposals for young audiences may be assessed. Two recent buzz phrases are '360 degree commissioning' and 'extending the narrative'; both referring to how elements of a TV programme can be expanded into a multi-platform environment. This is particularly true in the case of programmes designed to appeal to older children and young teenagers. The web content of shows like *The Sarah Jane Adventures* and *M. I. High*, with downloads, games and other interactive elements, helps to create a stronger connection with their audiences. If your great idea for a children's drama series has multi-platform potential, that may be an added selling point.

### Language and behaviour

Language must be used carefully in scripts for children. For the very young, sentences need to be simple and long words should be avoided. A word that is likely to be unfamiliar to the audience should be explained in context. Behaviour needs to be appropriate – characters can't be mean, tell lies or keep secrets from each other – and nothing should be depicted that could harm children if they attempted to copy it. Central characters can't be naughty, but secondary characters can, as long as issues are resolved. For instance, in *Grandpa in my Pocket* on CBeebies, it is all right if Grandpa is naughty, but not Jason, his grandson.

### Budgets

Live-action dramas and sitcoms for children are not simply cleaned-up versions of adult TV. Budgets are very much smaller, so they can't afford as many characters or sets and have to be economical with action sequences. Because of their focus, the casts will ideally be predominantly children rather than adults and the stories will inevitably be child-centred. However, this creates problems in production, as the number of hours children can work is strictly regulated. Night shooting, if allowed at all, will be strictly limited. The kind of series that would involve the same young actor in every scene – a junior version of Sam Tyler in *Life on Mars* for instance – should be avoided.

### Don't underestimate the audience

Children are sharper and quicker than adults and are very sophisti-cated viewers. They watch hours and hours of television and under-stand its visual language very well. Guy Hallifax reports that when *My Parents are Aliens* was being market-tested, the grown-ups who saw it didn't understand the premise and requested an introductory, scene-setting episode. The kids understood it immediately, because it had been covered in the animated title-sequence.

### The family audience

*Doctor Who* rediscovered the family audience in 2005. Its huge ratings and the success of other similar series demonstrate that shows that are suitable for children can still appeal to a very wide audience. In the cinema, the *Harry Potter* series, the *Toy Story* films and the critically acclaimed *UP* (nominated for best picture at the Oscars) have very successfully entertained children and emotionally involved adult audiences.

Julian Jones *(Merlin)* considers the important factors in a family drama to be:

> 'Heroism, humour, fun, action and above all warmth. The same rules apply in all drama – good stories and good relationships. I think magic is an additional bonus. When written down like that it all looks easy – getting that chemistry format right is very hard.'

He also adds that plots have to be 'sophisticated enough for an adult audience, but also comprehendible for a very young audience.'

'Family' shows do not have to be bland or cosy or banal, but they do have to be handled with sensitivity. Anything that could inspire 'imitative behaviour' needs to be approached with caution:

> 'I had a sequence where Arthur chucked Merlin into a boiling hot bath, it was very funny – but there was a concern that little Tommy might watch this, go upstairs for wash-time and chuck his sister into a scalding bath. It was a shame to have to re-write it, but these are the responsibilities you accept.'

Steven Moffat has not avoided tackling darker themes in *Doctor Who*. His first television success was the children's series *Press Gang* and he believes that everything can be done for a family audience. In an interview for *Hollywood Today* (24 October 2010) he says:

'To make something accessible to children only requires that you write it better. Seinfeld has said this. When he's got new material and he's working in the provinces, he's got lots of swearing in it to make the jokes work. As he refines the joke, there are no swear words at the end. You should be able to do a shock without gore, to do a joke without swearing, write about loss and loneliness and make it comprehensible to an 8 year old.'

Writing for a family audience can be very demanding, but Julian Jones stresses its rewards:

'It's not easy and good ideas do get rejected or altered – but that's the challenge and the beauty of the show. It's incredibly satisfying when you achieve a story that works for everyone.'

# 15 Script presentation

## How to present your script

You are not going to reach the television audience at all, if you don't captivate the script reader. It is therefore very important that the script is easy to read. This may seem obvious, but too often scripts contain too much information and too much set-up. Solid chunks of description between the lines of dialogue are very off-putting; plenty of white space on the page is a much more inviting prospect for the reader. Write clearly. A confused reader/audience is not going to be engaged with what is going on. There is a world of difference between confusing an audience and intriguing them, making them want to know more.

All scripts should be typed on one side of white A4-sized paper. Do not put important information in accompanying notes and outlines. It is very irritating – and time-consuming – for the reader to have to keep referring back to character breakdowns or whatever to work out who is who or what is what. After all, the television viewer will not have the benefit of your notes. Anything we need to know about the situation and the characters needs to be in the script and on the screen.

Presentation is important and it is not difficult to find out what a script should look like. A badly formatted script is very off-putting for a reader, who will be unlikely to persevere with it. All the time spent developing the characters and the story will be wasted. A correctly formatted script will demonstrate a professional approach, which is what a producer or agent is always looking for.

### Read scripts

The more scripts you can read, the better will be your understanding of what is required. The BBC writersroom website (www.bbc.co.uk/writersroom) has a number of produced scripts that can be downloaded. These include episodes of *EastEnders*, *Casualty*, *Doctor Who* and *Life on Mars*, as well as single dramas and sitcoms. Screenplays and television scripts can be found on numerous different sites on the internet. However, you need to make sure you are reading an actual script and not simply a transcript – a lot of scripts on 'fan' sites for individual series will be these. Some of the scripts you find will be shooting scripts that will contain information such as camera shots, which should not feature in the writer's draft. Most published scripts, unless the pages are full-size, will have been re-formatted to fit the dimensions of the book page so will not be a reliable template.

### Scriptwriting software

Formatting software is available, the industry standard and most popular programme being Final Draft. However, it is expensive. Celtx (www.celtx.com) can be downloaded free and is user-friendly scriptwriting software, although it is not as versatile as Final Draft. Script Smart, a set of Microsoft Word templates to help with formatting, is a free download available on the BBC writersroom website. However, you can set the margins manually and, as long as the finished article looks basically like a script with the dialogue and description in the right proportion and clear scene headings, then that will be acceptable to a reader. You will find downloadable notes on script formats for filmed and taped drama and studio-based audience sitcom on the BBC writersroom website.

## *Standard screenplay layout*

---

```
EXT. VENICE - DAY 1 1600

The year 1754.  Craning up the exterior of an elegant
townhouse, perfectly calm and leisurely; ivy, leading up to
the first floor, a balcony, a window...

A chair smashes through the window, from inside.  A man belts
out onto the balcony - CASANOVA, 29 y/o, a little, cheeky,
energetic man, in a hurry.  He whistles -

CUT TO the street.  A white horse gallops towards the house.

CUT TO CASANOVA, leaping up to balance on the balustrade.
CUT TO the horse, galloping.  CUT TO CASANOVA, jumping -

And missing.  The horse gallops past, CASANOVA slams on to
the ground.  Beat, then:
                    CASANOVA
          Bollocks.

Then he's up and running, full speed.  On the balcony, a fat
NOBLEMAN appears, yelling down;
                         NOBLEMAN
               Get him!  Don't just stand there,
               get him!

SERVANTS run out of the house, chasing CASANOVA.

CUT TO CASANOVA, blistering through the square, round
columns, over bridges, PEOPLE scattering in his wake, the
SERVANTS in pursuit.  And CASANOVA's grinning, loving it.

A NOBLEWOMAN - in a state of undress - appears on the
balcony, behind the NOBLEMAN.
                         NOBLEWOMAN
               Run, Jack!  Run!

The NOBLEMAN pushes her back inside.
                         NOBLEMAN
               Pietro!  That's the man!

PIETRO's part of a second group of SERVANTS, way across the
square.  He and his HENCHMEN start running, on a path to cut
off CASANOVA.

The NOBLEWOMAN reappears, carrying a big houseplant, with
which she gives her husband a good whack, then shouts to
CASANOVA:
                         NOBLEWOMAN
               Ruuuuun!




                                        (CONTINUED)
```

---

*Casanova* © Russell T Davies

## *Standard television layout*

---

1   INT. CHILDBIRTH CLASS (O.B.)   NIGHT

GARY AND A MASSIVELY PREGNANT
DOROTHY ARE IN A CLASS WITH OTHER
EXPECTANT COUPLES. THEY ARE SITTING ON
THE FLOOR TOGETHER.

THE KINDLY INSTRUCTOR HAS A HAND-
KNITTED VERSION OF THE FEMALE BIRTHING
ORGANS. SHE IS EASING A DOLL THROUGH AN
APERTURE.

INSTRUCTOR:   So this is the uterus and here is
the baby with its head engaged in the birth canal.

GARY:   (WHISPERED) How come yours doesn't
look like that?

DOROTHY:  Because I didn't knit my own groin.

THEY MUTTER OVER THE INSTRUCTOR, WHO
CARRIES ON TALKING IN THE BACKGROUND.

GARY:   You know they shave patients before
operations - are they going to shave you?

DOROTHY GIVES GARY A WEARY LOOK.

GARY:   I could do that, make myself useful-

DOROTHY:  We're having a home birth, nobody's
going to shave me.

GARY:   I could give you a quick trim, tidy you
up-

DOROTHY:  No, pay attention. You have to be ready
to deliver this baby in an emergency. I don't want you
panicking and trying to stuff the placenta back in.

GARY:   I've read up. It's our little baby. I know
all about it.

THEY SMILE AFFECTIONATELY AT EACH
OTHER.

DOROTHY:  So you don't still think test tube babies
have to smash their way out of their test tube to be born?

GARY:   I was joking.

---

*Men Behaving Badly* © Simon Nye

## Script formats

Scripts for television drama shot on film or single-camera video will use standard **screenplay format**. Multi-camera studio-based drama and situation comedy will use a variation of standard **television format**.

Unless it is a situation comedy, in which case it would probably be worth mastering the television layout, it would be appropriate to use standard screenplay layout for any unsolicited television script submission.

### *Screenplay format*

(The extract from *Casanova* on page 218 illustrates this.)

On an A4 sheet of paper, the left margin should be 1.5 inches, the right margin 1 inch, the top margin 1.5 inches and the bottom margin 1 inch.

The **scene heading** is in UPPER CASE and runs across the page from the left margin. In television scripts this is often underlined. There is a line space before the scene direction.

The **scene direction** is in lower case and runs across the page from the left margin. Character names mentioned appear in UPPER CASE. There is a line space before the character cue.

The **character cue**, the name of the character who is speaking, is in UPPER CASE and is indented 3.75 inches. (N.B. It is *not* centred.)

**Actor direction**, instructions on how the dialogue is delivered, is in brackets below the character's name or on a separate line within the dialogue and is indented 3.5 inches.

The **dialogue** is in lower case and is indented 3 inches and forms a column approximately 3 inches wide down the middle of the page. (N.B. It is *not* centred and *never* appears in inverted commas.)

The script should be typed in 12pt Courier. If these general instructions are followed, then a page of script will represent approximately one minute of screen time.

### Television layout

(The extract from *Men Behaving Badly* on page 219 illustrates this.)

Different television productions will have their own 'house rules', but will broadly follow these guidelines.

On an A4 sheet of paper the left margin should be 3.5 inches.

The **scene heading** is in UPPER CASE and runs across the page from the left margin.

The **scene direction** is in UPPER CASE and runs across the page from the left margin. The script is usually double-spaced.

The **character cue** is in UPPER CASE and is underlined.

The **dialogue** is in lower case and runs across the page from the left margin. It is usually double-spaced.

Each new scene starts on a new page. Thus, a full page of script in this format will last between 30 and 40 seconds.

## Scenes

Scripts are divided into scenes. A scene can be defined as an event happening in continuous time in a specific location. If either the time or the location changes, there is a new scene.

A scene will contain:

- a scene heading (or 'slug line') indicating where and when it is set
- scene directions describing the location, the characters when they first appear and the action taking place
- character(s) – (but not always)
- dialogue – (but not always).

### Scene headings

> INT. SEMINAR ROOM, UNIVERSITY – DAY 1
> EXT. CITY STREET, MANCHESTER – NIGHT 2

A scene is always INTERIOR or EXTERIOR, which is written as INT. or EXT. on the left of the scene heading. This applies whether your characters are in space, heaven, valhalla, a room, a desert, a spaceship, a cave or a tent.

The scene is either inside or outside. Incidentally, if your scene is in a car, it is written as INT. even though the car is outside.

The **specific location** is always identified and, if necessary, the **general location**. It's also important that the information is consistent. Don't refer to SEMINAR ROOM and then in a later scene CLASSROOM, if it's the same place.

Scenes are DAY or NIGHT, which is written on the right of the scene heading. But DAWN, MORNING, MIDDAY, AFTERNOON, DUSK, LATE EVENING, MIDNIGHT are acceptable, if there is a good reason to use them.

You can illustrate the time of day through description. However, a script set over one day or a shift *(Casualty)* may have a clock in the scene heading:

1) INT. CUBICLE DAY 1 10.15
2) INT. RECEPTION DAY 1 10.32

Scenes will have **day numbers**:

EXT. GARDEN DAY 1 (OR NIGHT 1)

Day numbers are important to establish the timescale of the script. The writer sets the timescale. Each time the script advances in time it has a new day number.

Day numbers assist the production – a character may appear in the same location (office, bedroom, garden) over a period of story days and their appearance or clothing may change or the setting may alter. In production-cost terms it is economical to shoot *all* scenes that take place in a single location in a block i.e. all together.

**Days** although numbered in consecutive order (1, 2, 3, etc.) do not themselves have to be consecutive.

You may advance your story over a full week so your day numbers will be consecutive – 1, 2, 3, 4, 5, 6, 7.

Or

Your drama leaps forward in time – it starts on Monday and then continues on Thursday – but on screen these will appear as DAY 1 and DAY 2.

Time that passes off-screen is not given a day number! It does not exist.

Identify FLASHBACKS or FLASHFORWARDS – write these in your scene heading and then write at the end of the scene 'end flash-back'. Flashbacks or flashforwards will not necessarily have day/night numbers – but an indication of a time earlier or in the future.

The *Casanova* script cuts between scenes with the young Casanova in 1754:

1) EXT. VENICE STREET – DAY 1

and scenes with the older Casanova in 1798:

2) INT. CASANOVA'S ROOM, CASTLE DUX – NIGHT A

The later scenes are differentiated by letters rather than numbers to avoid confusion.

Common reoccurring scenes that do not always have characters are **establishing shots**. These are scene-setters, telling the audience where we are. These can set up a location: is it a regular location (focal point)? Is it a **headquarters**? Is it telling the audience something? Is it a **courtroom/police station?** Or they can establish the mood/tone – waterside cabin/gloomy forest/barren planet:

3) EXT. NORFOLK COASTLINE DAY 1
Establishing shot of vast empty beach and stormy seas.

---

### A new scene

A change of location is a **change of scene**. If characters move between locations, it is a **change of scene**. An advancement in time is a **change of scene**, even if the location doesn't change. Consider an entrance or exit through a door to be a **change of scene**.

---

## *Scene direction*

### *Description of the location*

Description of the setting and location and any relevant information about the weather will go below the scene heading. Descriptions in a script should be kept to a minimum, you are not writing a novel. Nevertheless, there should be enough information for the reader to be able to visualise the scene. If the setting is something that will be familiar to them (Trafalgar Square or a country pub), there is no need to describe it at all. If it is beyond their experience (Heaven or Valhalla for instance), then it would be appropriate to include some description.

The first scene of *Casanova* is set in a Venice square in 1754. There is no description as it is safe to assume that anybody reading the script would have an idea what such a setting would look like. However, a few scenes later we are introduced to Casanova's room in Castle Dux in 1798. Here, appropriately, there is description:

> 'A high, vaulted bedroom, stacked with old books, his desk covered with yellowing handwritten pages. Stone walls and flagstones. It's cold and dusty, just the remnants of old luxury.'

You should not put anything in a script that will not be apparent to the audience. They won't be able to smell the scent of stale tobacco (unless one of the characters refers to it) or feel the cold draught under the door (unless one of the characters shivers). Nevertheless, it is advisable to create a sensory experience for the reader (your first audience). Jurgen Wolff suggests that a well-chosen detail (even if it won't be noticed by the audience) can bring something to life in the reader's mind.

*Description of the characters*

It is always helpful to give some indication of the age of characters, when they are first introduced, if it is not clear from the context. I once received a script about two guys on a road trip in Ireland and had assumed from the laddish banter in the dialogue that they were in their early twenties. Halfway through the script one of them mentioned he had a daughter just starting university. This resulted in a sudden mental gear-change for this particular reader! Two middle-aged guys behaving irresponsibly was a different story from the one I thought I was reading.

Russell T Davies, as well as giving the age of his characters, always uses a couple of appropriate adjectives to describe them. The 29-year-old Casanova is 'cheeky' and 'energetic', the 50-year-old cook is 'hefty' and 'rough', while the new 20-year-old maid, Edith, is 'quiet' but 'cleverer than those around her'. This is all that is needed for the reader to get an instant handle on them. Longer character descriptions are unnecessary, slow down the reader and get in the way of the unfolding action.

Stating that a character is very good-looking (or handsome, or a hunk, or fit, or stunning) will be enough for the reader to visualise their *own* ideal of beauty, you don't need to paint a picture in words for them.

Unless there is a specific story reason or idiosyncratic character reason for doing so, you do not need to describe what your characters are wearing.

As a general rule both for location description and character description, if something is *important*, mention it. If it's *unimportant*, leave it out.

*Description of the action*

At the top of every scene below the scene heading and before any dialogue, there should be a brief description of what is happening and who is there. In other words what we can see on the screen.

INT. WINE BAR. DAY 1

A crowded city bar at lunch-time. MATT and LIZ, with their drinks, elbow their way through to the only empty table.

All description of action should be in the present tense – it is happening now – and should be precise and not lengthy. Long paragraphs of description are difficult to read and should be avoided. Break them up into shorter sections, which are easier on the eye. Make each word count and where possible use expressive verbs. In a chase sequence Russell T Davies chooses his words carefully to convey energy and excitement – Casanova 'belts' out onto the balcony and is soon 'blistering' across the square – and favours dashes rather than full stops.

**Camera shots**

Camera shots and angles should not feature in your script. Leave the direction to the director and concentrate on telling the story. You want the reader to experience what you are describing as if they are watching it on the screen – camera shots are intrusive, clutter up the script and are distracting.

You can focus the audience's attention by the way you present the scene and the elements in it. If a specific detail is mentioned in the script, the director will feature it. 'A single tear runs down her cheek', 'a gloved hand knocks on the window', 'a half-empty bottle of pills is on the bedside-table' would all imply a close-up. If it is crucial to the story that something is shot in a particular way, then mention it, but don't overdo it. There is an argument in *Casanova* between the older Casanova and the cook, who slings a ladle-full of sauce at him. A note in the script reads '(Much of this played off EDITH, shocked)'. Edith, the new kitchen maid, is not actually involved in the conversation, but Russell T Davies makes it clear that the audience must be aware of her reaction to it.

### Actor direction

Actors, like directors, do not like being told how to do their job. However, there are occasions when it is necessary to state how a line is to be delivered if it is not clear from the meaning:

> NICK
>
> (sarcastically)
>> I'm really pleased to see you.

or who in the scene is being addressed:

> NICK
>
> (to CHARLOTTE)
>> Can I have a quiet word?
>
> (to MATT and LIZ)
>> Would you excuse us a moment?

These directions are placed in brackets on a separate line. Brackets should only be used for specific instructions regarding the delivery of the dialogue; they should not be used for any action directions.

### Dialogue

If a character's dialogue is interrupted by action directions, when they resume speaking the character cue should be repeated followed by (CONT'D):

GERALD

Wait a minute. 'Davey.' Not her Davey?
Dead Davey? It can't be . . .

GERALD runs to a desk, scrabbles about in a drawer, pulls out an old photo of KATE and DAVEY, holds it up next to DAVEY, looks from one to the other.

GERALD (CONT'D)
. . . But it is. This is awful. This is terrible.
You're alive.

(*My Favorite Husband*, Martin Cohan, Blake Hunter and Richard Sparks)

If only one line of directions interrupts the dialogue, it is not necessary to repeat the character cue:

GERALD

Wait a minute. 'Davey.' Not <u>her</u> Davey?
Dead Davey? It can't be . . .

GERALD picks up a photo, looks from one to the other.

. . . But it is. This is awful. This is terrible.
You're alive.

If there is dialogue that is spoken by a character in the scene who isn't actually on the screen – for example speaking from an adjoining room – their character cue is followed by (O.S.), meaning off-screen:

GERALD (O.S.)

or alternatively in TV scripts (O.O.V.), meaning out of vision.

If there is dialogue that is spoken by a character who isn't in the scene at all, as a narrator, or there is dialogue that is spoken by a character in the scene that is not heard by the other characters, in other words we are hearing their thoughts, their character cue is followed by (V.O.), meaning voice-over:

GERALD (V.O.)

(V.O.) is also used when a character can be heard via a mechanical device like a radio or a telephone.

All these 'rules' make a script easier to read and avoid confusion.

> 'Correct presentation and layout (format) are the first essential steps to selling your screenplay.'
> *Ray Frensham*

# 16 Writing is rewriting

If your script is going to be as good as it can possibly be, then inevitably it is going to have to be rewritten and rewritten and rewritten. Even when you have reached, or think you have reached, the final draft, it will still benefit from a polish here or a tweak there. Matthew Graham, speaking at the London Screenwriters' Festival, said:

> 'The first draft should be written with the head, subsequent drafts with the brain.'

Having written 35 drafts of the first episode of *Life on Mars*, he certainly knows what he is talking about! Russell T Davies, in the *Screenwipe* interview, reveals he is still rewriting in his head even when his work has been made:

> 'You're sitting there going "ouch!" . . . "I should have done it a different way" . . . you're rewriting it as you watch it transmitted almost . . . that never stops really. You just go "ouch!" the entire time!'

Tony Jordan will write 11 or 12 drafts of an episode of *Hustle*, honing it all the time, making it 'sharper, crisper, smarter'. Speaking on the same *Screenwipe* programme, Graham Linehan, creator of *The IT Crowd*, admits that writing the first draft can be so hard that once it is finished he doesn't want to change anything. However, he goes on to say:

'The truth is the second draft will become easier, the third draft easier still and by the fourth draft you'll be having such a good time, because by that stage you will have stripped away all the dead wood and you'll be adding in all these wonderful new jokes and the structure will work and everything will suggest something else.'

When you have completed a first draft, it is a good idea to put the script in your bottom drawer for a few days and then to come back to it with a fresh eye. Read it in one sitting without making notes, so that you get an overall impression of it. You might be surprised to discover what you think works and what doesn't. You will then need to consider the kind of questions a script reader will ask themselves about your script and ensure in subsequent drafts that any potential 'negatives' have been eliminated.

## The script report

A reader's report, or 'coverage', will consist of a synopsis of the script followed by an assessment based on a checklist, under different headings, and then a final verdict – a recommendation for serious consideration or rejection, based on the company's selection criteria. Different production companies and organisations will have their own checklists, but in general they will cover the following.

### Premise

What is the story? Whose story is it? What is at stake? What is it actually about? Is the theme clear? Does it have an original voice or way of looking at the world? Is it appropriate for its intended audience?

## Conflict

Is there any? Is there enough at stake? Are there different levels (inner, outer, societal) of conflict? Is there conflict in each scene? Is the central conflict resolved satisfactorily?

## Structure

What kind of structure is it? What is the plot? Is it full of cause and effect, of action and reaction? What are the subplots? Do they contribute to the main theme? Does the story start in the right place? Is it too simple? Is it too complicated? Does enough happen? Is each scene necessary? Are they in the right order? Are there scenes missing? Is there sufficient variety of pace? Are the climaxes in the right places? Does the end work?

## Characters

Are the characters engaging/interesting? Are they credible? Are they sympathetic? Are they clearly motivated? Are they consistent? Are they all distinctive? Do they develop? Is the number of characters workable? Are they all necessary? Do we care what happens to them?

## Dialogue

Does it reveal character? Does it move the story forward? Is it appropriate for this story? Is it characterised dialogue or stereotypical? Is it overwritten? Is every line necessary? Is there enough subtext or is it on the nose? Is the writer relying on the dialogue to tell the story?

### *Visual style*

Is the script using the visual nature of the medium to create a distinctive world? Is this apparent in the screen directions or use of filmic devices? Are these used appropriately? Does it have scenes/sequences that may interest a director? Does it have a workable number of locations?

These are all things to ask yourself as you rewrite.

## A second opinion

The key questions to ask of any script are 'Does the story make sense?' and 'Is the story clear?' These are not questions that are easy to answer when you have written it. You will be too close to it. Of course you will understand what is going on and why, but you may not have put it clearly enough on the page, even if it is in your head. This is why getting somebody, whose opinions you value, to read your first draft is very useful. You need another pair of eyes on it – a cool pair of eyes.

Even before they had the confidence to write scripts themselves, Laurence Marks and Maurice Gran started to go to Player-Playwrights (a London-based association of writers and actors, www.playerplaywrights.co.uk), which meets once a week and stages readings of members' scripts. After the reading there is always an audience discussion. The audience are not professionals, but Laurence recalls that in the 1970s there were two of them – one an industrial chemist and the other a civil servant – whose analytical criticism of drama was the best he has ever heard. Laurence and Maurice's earliest efforts were exposed to that audience and they are still involved in Player-Playwrights to this day. Laurence always stresses the importance of finding people you can trust to give you feedback on your script before you send it out.

## The rewrite

A common mistake that writers make is to assume that all the different problems in a first draft can be fixed in one massive rewrite. Ray Frensham advises tackling it in stages, each time concentrating on different aspects of the script and dealing with different questions in each rewrite. In *The Art & Science of Screenwriting*, Phil Parker makes the same point, suggesting five stages in the process.

- **The structural rewrite.** The focus is on making the dramatic structures work and ensuring that the audience has sufficient information to understand the story.
- **The character rewrite.** The aim of this rewrite is to ensure all the characters are credible and engaging enough to make them worth watching.
- **The scene/sequence rewrite.** With the overall dramatic structure and the characters in place, this rewrite addresses the smaller building blocks of the script. (A number of scenes may be rewritten and some added or taken away to provide a stronger sense of rhythm or tempo.)
- **The dialogue rewrite.** The aim of this rewrite is to ensure that all the dialogue is necessary and is character specific.
- **The polish.** Make it 'sharper, crisper, smarter' (Tony Jordan). Examine every line and every word of dialogue, description or action. Can it be improved? Can it be cut?

It is very easy to become attached to a line of dialogue or a particular scene and to lose sight of the overall picture. However, for the good of the script you have got to be prepared to 'kill your babies' (or 'murder your darlings', as literary critic and novelist Arthur Quiller-Couch originally phrased it) if they are not strictly necessary. It's not easy! (That's why they say you should always get somebody else to prune your roses, as you will never be ruthless enough!)

By addressing specifics in each rewrite, Ray Frensham stresses that each successive rewrite should improve your script, making it easier, more enjoyable and engaging to read.

There are no rules about how many rewrites you need to do, before you send your script out; you will do as many as you deem necessary to make it as good as it can be. Never submit a script with a letter stating 'I know it needs work'. Do the work first. However, regardless of how many times you have rewritten it, what you submit is always the 'first draft'.

Until it is actually in production (and even then it will change), every script is a work in progress, it is never really finished. After all, as an online dictionary defines it: a draft is 'a first or preliminary form of any writing, subject to revision'. Thus, by definition even a *final draft* is only the beginning! Television production is a collaborative process and many different people will have an input into your script's development and its passage to the screen. Rewrites are an inevitable part of the process.

### *Development* = *rewrites*

Writer Michelle Lipton, one of my ex-students, sets out in her blog (www.michellelipton.wordpress.com) the stages a TV series proposal might have to go through before it might be commissioned:

- reader/assistant at independent production company
- development producer at independent production company

- head of department at independent production company
- boss of independent production company
- reader/assistant at broadcaster/channel
- development producer at broadcaster/channel
- boss of development producer at broadcaster/channel
- commissioner at broadcaster/channel
- big boss of broadcaster/channel.

This not only demonstrates why the development process can take such a long time, but also how important it is to impress that initial reader on the bottom rung of the ladder. The other thing to bear in mind is that it is possible that everybody on the ladder will suggest 'improvements' (in other words rewrites) to the project before it is moved on to the next level.

Rewrites may not only be required to make a script or series treatment stronger, they may be required to make it more saleable. As Michelle writes:

> 'If there's a way of changing the tone, the structure or the length of the project to suit another channel, you start doing that. They might suggest your 2×60m BBC drama becomes a 3×45m ITV drama (3×60m with ads). Or maybe your 13×45m BBC drama series for Saturday night could be made darker and more adult to suit the current demand for 6×60m on weekdays at 9pm.'

### *Responding to notes*

Writing for television is not for the 'precious' prima donna or the sensitive artist, whose work is sacrosanct, it involves collaboration and compromise. After all, it is hard to imagine that rewrites didn't play a significant role in the development of Shakespeare's plays before they reached their first audience (and probably during their first run too). Nevertheless, a writer should be in a position to defend and preserve the integrity of what they have written. In her workshops, script analyst Clare Downs stresses that it is important that a writer is able to differentiate between suggestions that 'feed' and suggestions that 'hijack' their initial idea. In other words, good notes and bad notes.

Clare recommends enclosing a **note of intention** when a script is submitted. A note of intention explains briefly why you have written the script and what you are hoping to achieve in it. Thus, a reader will read your script, knowing and understanding exactly what you are trying to do. Any criticism is going to be informed criticism. Once a script editor or a producer becomes involved, if they too write down what they think the script is trying to achieve, what has drawn them to wish to develop it, then the writer knows that everybody is going in the same direction – is planning to make the same film or TV programme that they want to. See more in Julian's part on submissions on page 41.

In a widely circulated email critical of BBC Drama and published in *The Guardian* (15 July 2009), producer Tony Garnett wrote:

> 'Note giving is an art and a craft. It must happen in an atmosphere of earned trust and approval if it is to avoid defensive resistance. It must be specific and concrete. "Make it funnier" will not do. Nor will half understood jargon from a weekend screenwriters' course. Talk of "narrative arcs" and "epiphanies" and the writer will politely nod and go home to look longingly at the gas oven.'

Everybody in the business gets notes, not only the writers: the producers, directors, actors, casting directors, editors etc. They cannot be avoided. In order to avoid 'creative differences', it is important that there is mutual respect on both sides and that the writer is not only able to understand the note itself, but what is behind it. Even bad notes (and writers claim to get a lot of those!) can hint at something that is not working in the script, an area that needs to be looked at. A writer should always be prepared to listen.

### Bad notes

So how should you respond to 'bad' notes'? Barbara Machin offers the following advice:

'Writing is rewriting. And rewriting is responding to notes. And here lies the challenge. Editorial notes are not always good. Of course there is absolutely no definitive way to improve a script but the essence of a "good" note is that it creates a change which genuinely enhances the writer's intention, ideally excites the writer into enriching a character, improving a plot or honing story structure. You know when a note feels bad because it seems to derail where you want to go. And the answer is to be totally prepared before a meeting.

'Read and reread your script and ideally with a few days away from writing so you start to see it with fresh eyes. Know your script inside out so when debating you remember your original intention and don't get deflected. More often than not your intention is informed subconsciously so you have to excavate out the why of what you did. So then explain it and explain it well.

Often that will convert the "bad" note to a direction which will help. Or you will hear yourself solving the problem as you rehearse the argument. Try and keep an open heart and mind. Consider and listen to what is being suggested. Don't get angry. And don't feel the imperative to respond immediately.

'Allow yourself time to process the thought and maybe rather than literally doing what is suggested allow the thought to take you to a place where the question is answered another way. Your way. And ultimately if a note is clearly wrong headed you must resist and with finesse. In the end only you can respond to the note but to simply refuse rather than persuade will not endear you to your team. Responding to a bad note is a mixture of creativity and diplomacy. Of clear headed honesty and ingenuity.

'Finally if you don't have the luxury to be in the room with the note giver and you are responding to written notes – then write back when you don't agree. And keep writing. Don't just ignore. Use the power of email to debate your point and encourage dialogue. The process of simply typing your way through a note often solves the problem and convinces the editor. I often use the layer of communication as a postscript to a meeting. Going back over thoughts and raising new ones which emerge about material which wasn't spotted in the meeting. Ideally there is never a bad note, rather one you are sure isn't right. And one of your skills as writer is to hang onto your belief and find a way to say that clearly. And write it better.'

## The script editor

If your script goes into production or you are commissioned to write an episode for an existing series, you will be working closely with a script editor. The script editor is the vital link between the writer and the producer (and the rest of the production team) and has the sometimes difficult task of keeping both parties happy, of satisfying both parties' demands and constantly ensuring that at the end of the day the script is not only working, but is as good as it can be.

On an existing series, the script editor will ensure that the script is delivering exactly what the programme requires and that the writer has all the necessary background material that they need. Their intimate knowledge of all aspects of the programme will be a valuable resource for the writer. On one level, they are representing the audience – anticipating the problems the regular viewer might have, raising the awkward questions and criticisms they may raise and preventing them raising them later, when it is too late.

Different people involved in the production will have their own specific notes on each draft of the script. It is the script editor's role to filter these (some may be contradictory) and to convey them to the writer, so that the writer is only having to listen to one voice and not trying to serve a committee.

Script editing is a balancing act – in a lecture published in *Writing Long-Running Television Series*, Lilie Ferrari referred to it as 'tightrope walking' – between the demands of the production and the creative desires of the writer. Communication skills are very important, as well as tact and diplomacy, as Tony Garnett has pointed out.

### What writers think about script editors

I asked a number of writers what *they* thought made a good script editor. It was interesting, but perhaps not surprising, that they all gave similar answers.

The worst kind of script editor would appear to be the 'frustrated writer', who tries to impose their views on the script rather than offering objective and constructive criticism. The kind who says – 'I'd have done it differently' – 'Why is this room red? I'd have made it blue.' – 'Why did you call him that? I think he should be called this.' – and so on. The kind who wants to write the script for you or perhaps get their friends in to write it for you.

One writer told me he had recently delivered a first draft of a sitcom script. He was anxious to know if it was structurally sound, if it made sense, if it 'worked'. The first reaction he got was – 'I don't like the first joke on page three'. A bad script editor, in this writer's opinion, is 'nit picking' – fussing about irrelevant details, when the big picture needs to be addressed first.

One writer compared the script editor's role with that of an engineer – BMW (the writer) builds the car (the script), the script editor is the guy who tunes it and makes the engine hum. He also pointed out that whether the engineer liked the colour of the car, or whether it was the kind of car he would choose to drive, was irrelevant. He could still tune the engine and improve its performance. He offered another analogy. If his script was a piece of music, he would look to the script editor to listen to it and pick out the 'bum' notes.

One writer said that a good script editor will detect things in a script that the writer was already concerned about, but needed someone else to bring to their attention – they will also be able to pick up on things that the writer was only subconsciously worried about.

All the writers stressed that they thrived on encouragement and were far more open to criticism of their work if they received praise for the good bits first! They didn't expect, or want, the script editor to solve the problems for them, but appreciated constructive advice. Often 'the solution might come in the actual act of writing' and a sensitive script editor will know when to let the writer go away and trust them to work it out.

## Compromise and collaboration

The notes that you receive on a script, once it is in production, will not only relate to problems with the story or the characters. Changes may have to be made for practical ('*we can't shoot it as written*') or budgetary ('*we can't afford to shoot it as written*') reasons. As Tony Jordan put it at the London Screenwriters' Festival, 'Forty helicopters come over the horizon' in a script can soon become 'Twenty helicopters come over the horizon' and end up as 'One man with a gun comes over the horizon. Sound of helicopters.'!

Mark Bussell and Justin Sbresni, co-writers of *The Worst Week of My Life,* recall delivering a script and being told by their producer that there was just one word in it that was giving him a problem. They began to wonder which particular word in the dialogue had caused offence. However, the 'offending' word turned out to be in the sentence 'It is *snowing*'. As the story was set on Christmas Eve, they thought the snow would give it a more Christmassy feel. But the cost implications of having snow in *all* the exterior scenes (of which there were many) made the producer 'rather queasy'. He felt a lot better when they cut it, and they didn't feel they had compromised at all, as the snow wasn't crucial to the story or the comedy.

Sometimes, though, it is necessary for writers to resist requested changes. Mark and Justin did dig their heels in on another show when they were asked by the line producer to cut a zoo sequence from a script for cost reasons:

> 'We pointed out that the story wouldn't make sense and indicated the episode title on the front of the script – "*Zoo*".'

In the original script of an episode of Tony Marchant's *Holding On* there was a stabbing on the tube. London Transport was unwilling to allow such a scenario to be staged on one of their trains, so the producers had to look elsewhere. An appropriate tube carriage was sourced and there were plans actually to build track to run it on. It was going to cost a lot of money, which was added to the original budget, and would inevitably be a complicated shoot. As Kate Harwood, the script editor on the show, recalls, Tony Marchant made himself extremely popular when he announced that he would be very happy to rewrite the scene and set it in a phone box!

You may be asked to rewrite an exterior location scene as an interior studio scene or vice versa because of problems in the shooting schedule or to rewrite a scene because one of the actors is unavailable on the day it has to be shot. In that kind of situation you have to grit your teeth, get on with the job and do the best you can.

## Money on the screen

Writers do need to be aware of those aspects of a production that can be expensive in terms of time or money, but which will not necessarily enhance the viewing experience. However, producers can be more willing to spend money if it is going to be 'on the screen' (actors, costumes, locations, stunts etc.) and thus appreciated by the audience.

The two-hour pilot episode of *Lost* was reputed to have cost 14 million dollars and, according to *Variety* (7 August 2010), the 80-minute first episode of *Boardwalk Empire* cost 18 million dollars. British television budgets, by comparison, are tiny, but drama producers employ a similar strategy to make a lasting first impression.

The first episode of *Downton Abbey* is far more cinematic than the subsequent episodes. An expansive early morning sequence follows the servants through room after room after room, showing us a magnificent and elegant setting and establishing the well-oiled machine that is the efficiently organised Edwardian household. Although the later episodes are less lavishly presented, the show has made a strong first impression (with its echoes of *Gosford Park*) and of course it is the first episode that gets reviewed by the critics.

Tony Marchant says that a disproportionate amount of time and money is spent on the first episode of a series. He will write more than twice as many drafts compared to the subsequent episodes. The first episode needs to make an impact and to be 'sexy' in television terms – to be 'arresting'. The first five minutes are particularly important and this is where a lot of the budget will be spent.

If your series has an expensive sequence in it, it will be more likely to reach the screen if it is in the first episode and preferably in the first five minutes (the opening of *Casino Royale* is a good example of this audience-grabbing strategy in a feature film). However, less established writers do need to be careful not to appear to be too extravagant in their production demands.

## The mother of invention

Compromises in getting a script to the screen are not always to the detriment of the final product. The iconic five and a half minute steadicam shot in *Atonement* was the director Joe Wright's daring and ingenious response to a budget that could only afford 1,000 extras for one day. Originally scripted as a montage, the Dunkirk sequence would not only have required 30–40 set-ups, but consistent lighting and weather conditions. Quoted in the *Los Angeles Times* (28 December 2007), Joe Wright said:

> 'It was conceived out of necessity. We had one day with the extras and then the small issue of the tide coming in and washing away the entire set.'

Toby Whithouse, creator of *Being Human*, has said that the reason they have a door for death when a character in the show passes to the other side is that it was all they could afford, it was something they found in the props department. He hadn't started out with the idea of having 'death's door', but it has proved to be a powerful element of the series. Unable to afford CGI for the werewolf transformations, they have to use prosthetics and animatronics, which he feels actually makes the werewolf more 'real'. Equally the low budget means that the foundation of the show is character, the cheapest and most effective way of telling a story and engaging with an audience.

*Hattie,* a biopic about Hattie Jacques, was BBC4's most successful single drama to date. It was a period film on a limited budget, where Glasgow 2010 had to stand in for London 1966. Co-producer Seb Barwell says that rewriting was their principal weapon against budget problems. The writer, Stephen Russell, was on call throughout, some rewrites being made on the spot out of necessity. A three-scene sequence in a church hall became a single tracking shot on the church steps, after a fire alarm had shortened their shooting day. Writing in *Broadcast* (6 January 2011), Barwell adds:

'Some very effective script changes came through more patient work. The original script had a fact-based scene in which Hattie's dress caught fire during a TV pantomime that featured Spike Milligan and Frankie Howerd. The cast and stunt costs were too high for a scene that wasn't fully punching its weight. Between writer and director, it was rewritten as Hattie getting stuck in mid-air while testing a fly-wire. The image of Hattie alone, as a weightless fairy, captures her hopes and insecurities in a way that the burning dress never could, so a budget problem arguably helped to create one of the film's most resonant moments.'

There is always a balance between writing a script that is easily affordable (and possibly less demanding) and telling a story in the most effective way possible and presenting challenges to the director and the rest of the crew. Although you should not write a television script as if it has a feature film budget, you should not be afraid to be ambitious in your storytelling. Even though you will always have to be prepared to compromise if necessary, production teams will invariably come up with ingenious ways of transferring your creative vision to the screen. Nobody in television likes to say no unless they have to.

# Conclusion

## It's the way you tell 'em

Twenty years ago, interviewed by *The New York Times* (28 August 1991) about the success of the sitcom *The Upper Hand*, which Greg Freeman and I had adapted from the American show *Who's the Boss?*, I said:

> '*The Upper Hand* looks like a British car, but underneath the hood, it has a huge Buick engine.'

Unaware of its origins, (I am sure most of them at the time would have rejected the original series as 'too American') the ITV audience responded enthusiastically to the show's central relationship – that of the male housekeeper and his professional female boss – and the energy and pace of the unseen 'engine' that powered it. In *The Sunday Times* (4 September 2011) 20 years later almost to the day, I was interested to see Julian Fellowes saying something very similar:

> '*Downton Abbey* looks like a traditional period drama and everyone wanders around doing things right, but actually the structure is much more modern ... It's masses of different stories going on, little scenes you have to follow – it's very American. In their best popular drama, you jump from story to story. We do too. So I think it has a more modern energy, if I can say that, than a lot of the equivalent [period] shows.'

Behind its elegant facade, *Downton Abbey* is 'engineered' like *ER*, *NYPD Blue* and *The West Wing*.

This section of the book has been about the art and the craft of writing for a television audience. It's often what that audience doesn't actually see on the screen that can make the difference between success and failure. As Benji Wilson writes in *The Sunday Times* (4 September 2011):

> '*Downton Abbey* may entice viewers in with its window dressing – the costumes, the language, Maggie Smith's poison-tipped one-liners – but it's the engine of the drama, machine-tooled storytelling, that keeps them there.'

The successful television writer has to be both an artist and an engineer. You may have terrific stories to tell, but you won't make it in television without mastering the craft skills – the nuts and bolts – of how you're going to tell them. It is those skills that keep most writers in work, rather than their ability to keep on coming up with brilliant new ideas.

How do you acquire those skills?

- **Keep watching television.**
- **Keep reading scripts.**
- **Keep writing and rewriting.**

# Appendix

## Synopsis, outline and treatment for *Otters Reach* by Jim Hill

*Otters Reach* (see Chapter 11, page 152) is set in and around an RSPCA animal hospital in south-west England. It focuses on the investigative and preventative work of the RSPCA, featuring its front line uniformed inspectors, veterinary surgeons, undercover operatives and volunteers. It follows the RSPCA officers as they go about their daily task of dealing with the animals, their owners and the everyday people who live, work and holiday in their district. The *Otters Reach* province is an uneven mix of the urban and the rural which incorporates farmland, housing estates, coastlines, industrial parks, mountain ranges, building sites, abandoned mines and greyhound tracks.

## Otters Reach – synopsis

The whole of the OTTERS REACH unit is involved in identifying and prosecuting an illegal dog-fighting ring. An undercover operation, in which TOM plays a leading part, results in a police raid and the capture of the gang. Amongst those involved is a pet shop owner who LYNNE and SOPHIE are attempting to prosecute for trading in diseased rabbits. TOM'S actions prove both his dedication to his job and his courage, although ROY CHEAM is reluctant to offer any praise despite his growing respect for TOM. SAHANA assists TOM in his first court case and they secure a conviction. TOM is grateful for SAHANA'S support and advice and his attraction towards her is finally reciprocated. ROY'S attempts at heroics results in him being rescued by the fire brigade. The fire brigade officers supply a copy of the 'official' rescue video to be played back in the staff room for everybody to see, much to the amusement of everyone but ROY CHEAM.

## Otters Reach – outline

TOM HOLLY is keen to celebrate his first courtroom victory – the successful prosecution of an abusive animal owner but his plans are cut short by a call for help. TOM discovers a badly injured dog dumped by the side of the road. It has clearly been in an illegal dog fight. SAHANA treats it but does not hold out much hope for its survival. TOM is later called to the docks where customs officers have been covertly observing a boat. They suspect that it is smuggling fighting dogs into the country. CHIEF INSPECTOR JELLICOE, keen for publicity, has invited local journalist O'CONNOR to observe the Customs-led raid intended to arrest the boat owners. However O'CONNOR has a tip off about a forthcoming illegal dog fight and the Customs raid is called off in order for TOM to follow the imported dogs to their final destination. By trailing one of the targeted importers (KELLOWAY), TOM discovers the location of an illegal dog fight. This culminates in a full-scale police raid and arrests involving all the active inspectors from the OTTERS REACH branch. Meanwhile ROY CHEAM is rescued by the fire brigade when he becomes wedged in a church belfry while trying to tend to a trapped bat. A fire brigade training video eventually finds its way back to the OTTERS REACH sanctuary where it becomes popular tea-time viewing, much to CHEAM'S embarrassment. SOPHIE alerts SAHANA to a number of sick pet rabbits, all purchased from the same pet shop. SAHANA, along with CHEAM, investigate the pet shop but fail to substantiate the allegations that they are mistreating their animals. When CHEAM assists in the raid on the illegal dog fight he encounters the owner of the pet shop and ensures he is arrested and charged, allowing further action against the pet shop. LYNNE has to attend to a call to a sick parrot which, it transpires, has developed a chesty cough due to its owner smoking 80 cigarettes a day. LYNNE re-homes the parrot, only to be kept awake at night by its constant hacking!

*Here the A, B and C stories are separated out. (There is also a D story – some dramas have a fourth simple storyline).*

**A)** *Illegal dog fight – covert operations – police raid – arrests – all characters involved.*

**B)** *Pet shop trading in sick rabbits – secondary characters – but links into dog raid (**A** storyline) via pet shop owner.*

**C)** *CHEAM stuck in a belfry and a video shot that gets played at base.*

**D)** *Parrot with a smokers' cough.*

## *Otters Reach* – treatment

A battered car pulls to a halt in a country lane. The driver, KELLOWAY goes to the boot of the car and opens it. He lifts out an injured and bleeding dog and dumps it in the ditch at the side of the road. KELLOWAY drives off. The abandoned dog struggles to get up but cannot.

TOM HOLLY waits in the outer chamber of the magistrates' court. He paces up and down and when he does sit down he nervously fiddles with his cap. SAHANA appears to offer comforting words and reassure TOM that he has no worries about winning this case. SAHANA believes TOM has compiled an excellent evidence portfolio of pictures and statements. TOM relaxes a little and admires SAHANA'S business suit. She smiles in response, flattered, and explains that as an expert witness in a court case she is required to look her best. TOM is of the opinion that SAHANA always looks good.

LYNNE HARRIS is talking to Mrs CARRENA, a cleaning lady/ home help, but finding her accent a stumbling block. The problem is unclear but Mrs CARRENA is obviously worried as it concerns one of her clients Mrs TUTTON, an elderly housebound widow. It also appears to involve a bird of some sort. Mrs CARRENA manages to impersonate a parrot and then explains that this creature is in danger of either being choked or suffocated. LYNNE is a little confused but as Mrs CARRENA appears concerned and insistent LYNNE agrees to visit Mrs TUTTON. LYNNE also agrees to keep Mrs CARRENA'S name out of it.

ROY CHEAM is in church on a call. The VICAR, an overweight, cheery man, chats away to CHEAM as though he has known him for years. The VICAR explains that the church is undergoing extensive repairs and is quite blatant about the need to raise money and CHEAM realises that he is being asked for a donation. Skirting the issue, CHEAM gets back to the reason that he has been called out. Bats in the belfry. The vicar wants something done about them, something humane. CHEAM is more of the opinion just to exterminate them, better all round. The VICAR is shocked and CHEAM pretends he was joking. Given the location of the bats – at the upper most point of the church, CHEAM reluctantly agrees to take a look. CHEAM is hesitant. He's afraid of heights!

TOM is in court, at the summation of his first court case. SAHANA also present, as the professional witness. The defendant is found guilty, fined and banned from further animal ownership. TOM offers SAHANA a big smile. It's a great start to the day for him.

TOM wants to celebrate his courthouse victory. SAHANA has to get back to work. So does TOM, when a call to attend an injured dog comes through.

At the OTTERS REACH sanctuary SOPHIE is tending a sick rabbit belonging to a tearful child. The child's mother had recently purchased the rabbit as a gift from a pet shop and it became ill almost immediately. The pet shop owner refused any responsibility for the rabbit's condition and refused to give a refund or exchange. SOPHIE wants to keep the rabbit at the surgery in order to treat it.

CHEAM follows the VICAR up into the rafters. The VICAR is puffing and CHEAM offers to go on alone. The VICAR is insistent. He needs the exercise.

TOM is at the roadside tending the abandoned dog, discovered by a postman on his rounds. The dog is badly injured as a result of an illegal dog fight. TOM intends taking it to SAHANA'S surgery.

LYNNE is at Mrs TUTTON'S – she is a house-bound chain smoker and TV watcher. The place is thick with smoke. The ceiling and walls are nicotine stained. A parrot perches amongst the ashtrays, cigarette butts and empty packets. When Mrs TUTTON coughs, the parrot coughs. LYNNE tries to convince Mrs TUTTON that the parrot's health is at risk.

Mrs TUTTON thought the parrot would be good company but he repeats things more than the television.

The last section is up a ladder, through a small trap door and into the steeple top. CHEAM gingerly makes the climb and is pleased to be off the rickety ladder. The VICAR follows and gets his large bulk stuck in the trap door entrance. He hasn't been up here for some time. About three stone ago! His struggling kicks away the ladder and he is wedged, with a long drop below him. There is no other exit from the steeple. Except the scaffold. CHEAM'S mobile phone doesn't operate in this area. If they need help, he's going to have to go over the side.

SAHANA is stitching and bandaging the fighting dog while TOM looks on. Its injuries are serious and SAHANA doesn't give it much of a chance of survival.

CHEAM is out on the scaffold. Frozen to it. He can't move. From inside the steeple the trapped VICAR offers comforting words and the usual 'don't look down' advice.

SAHANA has placed the dog in a holding area. It sleeps. While scrubbing up SAHANA mentions the sick rabbit and the pet shop from which it was bought, PETS PARADISE. SAHANA believes the rabbit was sick when it was sold. TOM seems to remember a prosecution against the pet shop when he was a probationer in the region.

Chief Fire Officer BLAKE stands beside the fire engine watching CHEAM being rescued from the scaffold. He is highly amused. Meanwhile a fire fighter suggests leaving the VICAR for a few days until he has lost some weight. (A passing parishioner had phoned for help).

Once on the ground, CHEAM confronts BLAKE and requests that the incident isn't made public. BLAKE thinks it's a first; RSPCA officer rescued by Fire Brigade. It beats 'the cat in the tree story'.

LYNNE returns home to her family with the parrot. Her two teenage children insist that there are too many 'rescued' pets in the house and garden. Her children are bored with the feeding and cleaning routines for the hamsters, gerbils, rabbits and goldfish etc. They have outgrown cute pets and are into computers. They don't want the parrot. Nor does LYNNE'S husband, GERRY.

CHEAM tells TOM that he prosecuted PETS PARADISE, but before he got WRIGHT, the owner, to court the ownership and licence for the business was transferred to Mrs WRIGHT. The shop continued trading despite WRIGHT being found guilty. CHEAM wants to check this out himself and arranges to contact SAHANA.

CHEAM meets SAHANA at the pet shop. They go in together. Mrs WRIGHT greets them. Her husband is out on business. She denies selling the rabbit. They have no rabbits. CHEAM finds only empty rabbit cages that have been scrubbed clean.

When they leave CHEAM suspects that WRIGHT is out dumping the rabbits. CHEAM could organise an inspection of the pet shop but expects it all to be clean and tidy by the time that happens.

TOM is told to join Chief Inspector JELLICOE at the marina. When TOM arrives he meets O'CONNOR, pursuing a tip-off of his own.

Customs officers have been observing a recently arrived boat. At first they suspected drugs but now believe, having seen quantities of dog food taken on board, that animals are being smuggled ashore. They want assistance when they board the boat for inspection.

JELLICOE is keen to assist and expects a photo opportunity if the inspection is positive.

O'CONNOR tells them that his inside information details a forthcoming illegal dog fight. The dogs on the boat may have been imported especially for it.

O'CONNOR and TOM argue that an inspection may net them some dogs, but observation coupled with O'CONNOR'S contacts may lead them to some of the organisers.

JELLICOE and the Customs Officers agree to delay an inspection. TOM volunteers to keep watch on the boat. O'CONNOR wants to bring in local TV. This is the chance for him to broaden his career horizons. He promises JELLICOE front page billing and a TV interview.

TOM, in plain clothes, makes a tour of the marina and comes across the PETS PARADISE van in the visitors' car park.

TOM'S watch is relieved by CHEAM. TOM tells CHEAM about seeing the PETS PARADISE van. CHEAM sees the arrival of prospective customers. He recognises KELLOWAY, whom he has successfully prosecuted in the past. (KELLOWAY earlier abandoned the injured dog in the ditch).

The Customs Officers are concerned about the consequences of delaying an inspection and possible arrests, but O'CONNOR phones through with a time and a location for the dog fight.

JELLICOE has police co-operation to raid the illegal dog fight. Units will be put into place earlier in the day. SAHANA has been asked to attend to take care of any animals that are seized.

The location of the fight is an illegally constructed 'fighting ring' in a disused farm building.

Evening: RSPCA officers and police are in hiding, observing the arrival of the fighting dogs, their handlers and the punters. CHEAM sees the PETS PARADISE van and KELLOWAY.

O'CONNOR has a two man TV news crew with him.

Customs Officers board the boat and arrest the owner.

A swooping police helicopter announces the start of the raid. The fleeing punters abandon their cars and scatter across the fields as the roads are blocked by police vehicles.

The dog owners are arrested and CHEAM confronts Mr & Mrs WRIGHT of PETS PARADISE.

TOM is knocked over by a fleeing figure and gives chase into the forest, only to be confronted by KELLOWAY, armed with a commando style knife. TOM backs off and KELLOWAY is snared around the neck with a dog pole by LYNNE.

Returning to the 'fighting ring' they find JELLICOE being interviewed by O'CONNOR and the dogs being rounded up. SAHANA treats an injured animal.

The next day at RSPCA HQ JELLICOE is complimentary of his team at the local TV news de-briefing.

TOM watches as SAHANA returns the rabbit to the little girl. It has made a full recovery.

So has the injured fighting dog. It survived but faced being put down because it was not registered. SAHANA tells TOM of her contact, a man in Scotland with a small private estate, who 'de-trains' fighting dogs and gives them sanctuary. The dog has gone there.

CHEAM is summoned into JELLICOE'S office where he finds the HQ staff and members of the animal shelter assembled around the video/TV. (No sign of JELLICOE).

LYNNE loads the video, dropped off earlier by the Fire Brigade Video Unit. It plays. CHEAM is embarrassed (and angry) as everyone laughs at footage of him being 'rescued' from a church scaffold.

CHEAM is driving along narrow and twisting country roads. On a long open stretch he finds himself forced off the road by an oncoming tractor, driven by DOUG JACKLY (a constant adversary). JACKLY gesticulates obscenely as he passes CHEAM'S van. CHEAM curses under his breath.

END EPISODE

© JIM HILL

# Glossary

**Above-the-line**
Items on the budget of TV show or film covering script (and if applicable underlying rights like a book), director, producer and lead actors. (See also **Below-the-line**.)

**A-list writer**
A writer recognised as bankable, i.e. will attract investment or a broadcast commitment; usually with a substantial track record.

**Antagonist**
A character who opposes the **protagonist**.

**Assignment**
A commission, being hired to write a draft of a script.

**Associate producer**
A credit often given to someone like a writer or investor as a gesture, or to the assistant of the producer. Has relatively little power but is able to keep on top of what's happening.

**Backdoor pilot**
A stand alone, self-contained single drama which could be a prequel to a series. Instead of writing episode one of a new series (approximately 50 minutes) a backdoor pilot can also work as a stand alone TV movie and is usually 90 minutes.

**Back-story**

What has happened to the characters in the past before the action of the current story.

**BARB**

Broadcasters Audience Research Board, the main provider of television audience measurement in the UK.

**Below-the-line**

All the costs of the budget apart from **above-the-line** items.

**Bible**

A reference document for writers on a television series containing information on the format, the 'rules' of the show, the characters, episode storylines, sets and locations, etc.

**Calling card scripts**

Scripts that demonstrate the writer's ability and range. Used to get work on other projects.

**Ceiling**

Writers' fees are sometimes defined as a guaranteed minimum or maximum depending on the budget. The maximum is called the ceiling. (See also **Floor**.)

**Certified budget**

An official budget given to all appropriate parties by the accountant who certifies that on the first day of principal photography the production is expected to cost x.

**Chain of title**

This identifies all the copyright holders of any copyright work. So if a TV production is based on a novel the producer needs clear chain of title proving that they have purchased the novel from the copyright owner of the novel.

## Completion bond

A kind of specialised insurance that investors require before they will put their investment in: the completion bond company can take over the production if it is not on time or on budget and ensure that it is completed to the investors' relative satisfaction.

## Contingency budget

If a film is going to cost £1 million to make and every penny of that is needed then the budget for the film might need to be 5% higher than that because investors like there to be a contingency amount raised in case things go wrong.

## Co-producer

A vague term that covers all sorts of individuals: co-producers can be responsible for bringing in finance and actually handling some of the production but sometimes a co-producer credit is given as a gesture.

## Copyright

Copyright subsists in the material form of anything written, drawn, sculpted etc. In the EU it lasts for 70 years from the end of the year of the death of the author. The *Writers' & Artists' Yearbook* has a very clear description of copyright.

## Copyrightable

Ideas are not copyrightable. If written down in considerable detail then that is copyrightable. Ideas can be protected using the breach of confidentiality law.

## Credits

If you write something which gets produced you should get a credit. Your credits should go onto **IMDb**. Credits are often given more easily than payment but in general try to get both.

## Cut-off

Producers require the right to fire writers if they are not getting material they find acceptable and the point at which they can fire them is called cut-off. It is normal in most contracts.

## Deal memo

A deal memo is a contract but a very abbreviated one and lawyers generally don't like them. However, if the situation is relatively simple, a well-drawn deal memo is a good compromise.

## Elevator pitch

In theory it's a pitch short enough to be able to be made between the ground floor and whichever floor you're getting out at in an elevator!

## Exercise

The word exercise in a writer's contract refers to the point at which the rights which have previously been optioned are now purchased. The phrase is that 'the option is exercised'.

## Exposition

Information the audience needs in order to understand a story. How the 'undisturbed routine of life' of the main character is set up before the **inciting incident.**

## First day of principal photography

The day on which the filming or taping of a programme starts.

## Floor

Floor is the guaranteed minimum in an agreement that the writer will get paid. (See also **Ceiling.**)

## Format

The overall concept and episodic structure of a television series.

**Genre**
The type of television programme. Within the overall television genres (drama, comedy, children's etc.), there are many sub-genres (the detective show, situation comedy, animation etc.). The phrase 'genre TV' is often used to describe science fiction, horror and fantasy.

**Greenlight**
This is the term used usually when a broadcaster having approved the script and the budget gives the greenlight that the production can now go ahead.

**High concept**
Describes a film or television series, whose **premise** can be communicated in a single phrase or simple sentence (e.g. *Snakes on a Plane*).

**Holdback**
This refers to reserving certain rights such as stage or radio or publishing rights when doing a script deal. It can also refer to the period of time that these rights are held back for.

**IMDb**
Internet Movie Database: generally accepted as the fount of all data about every production, although not totally reliable.

**Inciting incident**
The event that starts a story by throwing the main character out of balance. Otherwise known as the 'point of attack' or 'the hook'.

**Miniseries**
This is a television series that could run from three episodes upwards. If it's more than six or seven it is usually called a series or the first series followed by a second one of a further six or seven episodes. In America a series is more likely to be 22 episodes.

## On the nose

Dialogue that states the obvious; characters tell each other exactly how they feel and what they are thinking, leaving no room for **subtext**.

## Outline

More detailed than a **synopsis**, with more emphasis on character, tone and theme.

## Overnights

**BARB** releases overnight **ratings** every morning at 9.30am. These are based on the previous day's live viewing and 'same day playback' figures. The published weekly **ratings** are based on seven-day consolidated figures (taking account of the delayed viewing of recorded programmes).

## PACT

Producers' Alliance for Cinema and Television: this is the 'union' that negotiates on behalf of its producer members and many of the Writers' Guild agreements are with PACT.

## *Per diems*

If you are either on set or travelling to a location you can get paid 'expenses'. These usually cover incidentals like phone calls and snacks and drinks and can be as little as £20 a day. They're worth getting if you can.

## Pilot

A 'prototype' episode of a series designed to sell it to a network commissioner. Usually transmitted as the first episode, unless there are major changes. (See also **Backdoor pilot**.)

## Post-watershed

Programmes transmitted after 9pm. (See also **Watershed**.)

**Premise**

The fundamental idea, on which a story or series is based.

**Producer's net profits**

When revenue from a film or TV programme comes into a producer, that revenue is their gross; they have to pay various people and will eventually be left with net profits (seldom more than 20% of the production's profits). The writer normally gets a small share (2%–5%) of the producer's net profits.

**Protagonist**

The main character in a story.

**Ratings**

Data relating to the size of television audiences measured by **BARB** and published every week.

**Rebrief fee**

If a writer is asked to write a draft and is given notes and follows the notes and the producer then changes their mind and wants them to do something different, it's sometimes possible to negotiate a rebrief fee, which is not additional money on top of the fee but is bringing forward some of the money due because the writer is being asked to do something over and above what they were originally asked to do.

**Residuals**

Residuals refer to earnings that may be made subsequent to the payment of the full fee: profits could be residuals; selling subsidiary rights to another company or another country could be residuals. A sale of a TV episode to a foreign country could result in residual payments (if the original fee was not a complete buyout of those residual payments).

**Reversion**

Normally the producer acquires the right to make a film or a TV programme and they have a limited period of time in which to make it. Five or seven years is common. If they fail to make it within that period of time then the rights 'revert'. Paperwork may be necessary in order to enact this.

**Scene by scene**

A scene by scene breakdown is the equivalent of a step outline for a feature film. It contains details of every scene in a story.

**Schedule**

The running order of programmes on a television channel.

**Serial**

This is a long running storyline like a soap where at the end of an episode certain things may be resolved but the majority are not. See **series**.

**Series**

This is a long running show in which there is usually a self-contained story for each episode. However, there may be serial elements usually relating to the regular characters that can run through many episodes.

**Showrunner**

Executive producer and head writer of a series, usually its creator.

**Slot**

A specific time period in the **schedule**.

**Spec script**

Spec stands for 'speculative': in other words a script written by a writer on their own without any form of commission. Also used for **calling card script**.

**Subtext**

The actual meaning (apparent to the audience) behind what the characters are saying or doing.

**Synopsis**

A summary of what happens in a story.

**Trades**

This refers to trade papers such as *Broadcast* magazine, *Screen International*, *Variety*.

**Treatment**

More detailed than an **outline** and written in the present tense, it covers the full story sequence with everything resolved. It should make the reader want to read or commission the script.

**Turnaround**

Turnaround and **reversion** often go together. The turnaround clause refers to the terms under which the rights can revert.

**Underlying rights**

If a script is based on a book or a short story or a play the underlying rights refer to the source material for the script and normally need to be acquired by the producer.

**Watershed**

9pm. Material unsuitable for children should not be shown before 9pm or after 5am.

**Writers' Guild minimums**

The Writers' Guild has negotiated with broadcasters and PACT the minimum fees that should be paid for work done by a writer. These fees are a sensible basis for relatively new writers to start negotiating from. Established writers normally get fees higher than the minimums.

# Resources

This is a select list of resources mentioned in the book: these are accessible and provide useful information. Check their websites.

**HW Fisher**
Tax advice link for writers. A major accountancy firm that specialises in the media and in writers. Includes a very useful tax guide for writers.
www.hwfisher.co.uk/index.php/publications/260-authors-and-freelance-journalists-a-guide-to-tax-2011

**BBC writersroom**
BBC's resource for new writing and first port of call for unsolicited material. Reads for all BBC departments and runs a variety of schemes targeted at all levels of writer.
www.bbc.co.uk/writersroom

**Trade papers**
*Broadcast* for television; *Screen International* for film.
www.broadcastnow.co.uk
www.screendaily.com

**BFI** (British Film Institute)
Now the lead body for film in the UK, the BFI has many initiatives to help writers and filmmakers develop their projects.
http://industry.bfi.org.uk

**Skillset**

A UK-wide industry body that provides skills training to people in creative industries.

www.skillset.org

**PACT**

UK trade association protecting the commercial interests of independent feature film, television, digital, children's and animation media companies.

www.pact.co.uk

**WGGB** (Writers' Guild of Great Britain)

The UK trade union for writers of TV, radio, theatre, books, poetry, film, online and video games.

www.writersguild.org.uk

**London Screenwriters' Festival**

Biggest screenwriters festival in the UK; with over 100 industry speakers and many more producers, directors and screenwriters in the audience, this is an unmissable networking opportunity.

www.londonscreenwritersfestival.com

**The Script Factory**

Dedicated to finding and developing new screenwriting talent, as well as putting it in touch with the industry. Runs many events and training schemes.

www.scriptfactory.co.uk

**IMDb** (Internet Movie Database)

The pre-eminent film and television resource for cast and crew lists, box office figures, production company information and much more.

www.imdb.com

## Rocliffe Forum

A forum for new writing talent that stages performances of scripts in front of industry experts at BAFTA.

www.rocliffe.com

## Red Planet Prize

Prize run by Red Planet Pictures in association with Kudos. The winner receives a £5,000 cash prize and entry into a mentoring scheme. Over a dozen writers found through the scheme are now in development with Red Planet and Kudos.

www.redplanetpictures.co.uk

## Twelvepoint.com

Online incarnation of *ScriptWriter* magazine, Europe's leading journal on writing for the screen.

www.twelvepoint.com

## Writers' & Artists' Yearbook

Industry advice for writers and artists as well as assistance throughout the writing process.

www.writersandartists.co.uk

# About the authors

**Julian Friedmann** is co-owner of the Blake Friedmann Literary Agency (www.blakefriedmann.co.uk) and was the publisher of *ScriptWriter* magazine, which became the online resource for writers at www. twelvepoint.com. He represents both book and scriptwriters and also acts as executive producer for and with clients. He has taught at universities and film schools all over the world, is the author of *How to Make Money Scriptwriting* and editor of two volumes on Writing Long-Running Television series. He co-designed the MA in Television Scriptwriting at De Montfort University and PILOTS, an initiative for developing long-running television series for the EU MEDIA Programme. He is Senior Advisor to the London Screenwriters' Festival.

**Christopher Walker** is the programme leader for De Montfort University's MA in Television Scriptwriting, which he co-designed. He was the Head of Central Independent Television's Script Unit and later the Creative Executive of CTCP (Columbia TriStar Central Productions). As a television producer, he was responsible for all 94 episodes of the ITV sitcom *The Upper Hand*, which featured Joe McGann, Diana Weston and Honor Blackman. He also produced *Sob Sisters*, written by Andrew Marshall, for Central Television and has developed comedy projects for Carlton and the BBC. He teaches on the MA Creative Writing at York St John University and has given lectures in the USA and Germany on situation comedy. He has been a trustee of Nottingham Playhouse and is the Vice Chair of Writing East Midlands.

# Acknowledgements

With many thanks to all those clients who wrote the work I was able to negotiate contracts on, and all the producers who pushed us to test the bounds of our negotiating strategies.

I would also like to thank my colleagues, Conrad Williams and Daniel Nixon, for their help with the book.

*Julian*

I should like to thank all my past and present MA TV Scriptwriting students at De Montfort University for asking all the right questions and all the MA's visiting speakers, many of whom are quoted in this book, for providing the answers.

I am particularly indebted to my colleague, Jim Hill, for all his help and encouragement and also for allowing me to use his workshop notes and the *Otters Reach* material.

Many thanks also to Matthew Graham, Andy Hamilton, Julian Jones, Barbara Machin, Jimmy McGovern, Tony Marchant, Simon Nye, John Peek, Neil Penswick, Justin Sbresni and John Yorke for their help and contributions.

Thank you to Nicola Shindler, Red Production Company, for permission to use the extract from Russell T Davies' *Casanova* and

Beryl Vertue, Hartswood Films, for permission to use the extract from Simon Nye's *Men Behaving Badly*.

*Christopher*

We would also like to thank Hugh Brune and Alison Yates and the team at Crimson Publishing for all their help with this book.